BUILDING A FOUNDATION FOR SOUND ENVIRONMENTAL DECISIONS

Committee on Research Opportunities and Priorities for EPA
Board on Environmental Studies and Toxicology
Water Science and Technology Board
Commission on Geosciences, Environment, and Resources
National Research Council

National Academy Press
Washington, D.C. 1997

NATIONAL ACADEMY PRESS 2101 Constitution Avenue, N.W. Washington, DC 20418

NOTICE: The project that is the subject of this report was approved by the Governing Board of the National Research Council, whose members are drawn from the councils of the National Academy of Sciences, the National Academy of Engineering, and the Institute of Medicine. The members of the committee responsible for the report were chosen for their special competencies and with regard for appropriate balance.

This report has been reviewed by a group other than the authors according to procedures approved by a Report Review Committee consisting of members of the National Academy of Sciences, the National Academy of Engineering, and the Institute of Medicine.

This study was supported by Contract Number 68W40044 between the National Academy of Sciences and the U.S. Environmental Protection Agency. Any opinions, findings, conclusions, or recommendations expressed in this publication are those of the author(s) and do not necessarily reflect the view of the organizations or agencies that provided support for this project.

Library of Congress Catalog Card No. 97-67451
International Standard Book No. 0-309-05795-7

Additional copies of this report are available from: National Academy Press 2101 Constitution Avenue, N.W. Box 285 Washington, D.C. 20055 800-624-6242 202-334-3313 (in the Washington Metropolitan Area) http://www.nap.edu

Cover art created by Carrie Mallory. Ms. Mallory received her Bachelor of Fine Arts Degree from the Cooper Union for the Advancement of Science and Art. She takes many of her themes from the natural world and she has provided covers for many National Research Council reports.
Copyright 1997 by the National Academy of Sciences. All rights reserved.

Printed in the United States of America

COMMITTEE ON RESEARCH OPPORTUNITIES AND PRIORITIESFOR THE ENVIRONMENTAL PROTECTION AGENCY

RAYMOND C. LOEHR, *Chair*, The University of Texas, Austin
SANDRA O. ARCHIBALD, University of Minnesota, Minneapolis
JOHN I. BRAUMAN, Stanford University, California
JOHN D. BREDEHOEFT, The Hydrodynamics Group, La Honda, California
GEORGE P. DALTON, The Procter & Gamble Co., Cincinnati, Ohio
KENNETH L. DEMERJIAN, State University of New York-Albany
NINA V. FEDOROFF, The Pennsylvania State University, University Park
ROLF HARTUNG, University of Michigan, Ann Arbor
JAMES F. HAYS, National Science Foundation, (retired), Arlington, Virginia
CHARLES E. KOLB, Aerodyne Research, Inc., Billerica, Massachusetts
JUDITH McDOWELL, Woods Hole Oceanographic Institution, Massachusetts
JUDITH L. MEYER, University of Georgia, Athens
CHARLES R. O'MELIA, The Johns Hopkins University, Baltimore, Maryland
*MICHAEL J. WILEY, University of Michigan, Ann Arbor
GARY M. WILLIAMS, American Health Foundation, Valhalla, New York
ROY L. WOLFE, Metropolitan Water District of Southern California, Los Angeles
LILY YOUNG, Rutgers University, New Brunswick, New Jersey
THOMAS W. ZOSEL, 3M Company, St. Paul, Minnesota

Staff

MORGAN GOPNIK, Study Director
SHEILA DAVID, Senior Staff Officer
DAVID POLICANSKY, Senior Staff Officer (until 10/96)
ADRIENNE S. DAVIS, Senior Project Assistant (until 3/97)
STEPHANIE VANN, Project Assistant (as of 2/97)
ANGELA BRUBAKER, Research Assistant
ANNE McCASLAND-PEXTON, Intern

---

* Michael J. Wiley resigned on 10/15/96 due to scheduling conflicts.

BOARD ON ENVIRONMENTAL STUDIES AND TOXICOLOGY

PAUL G. RISSER, *Chair,* Oregon State University, Corvallis
MAY R. BERENBAUM, University of Illinois, Urbana
EULA BINGHAM, University of Cincinnati, Cincinnati, Ohio
PAUL BUSCH, Malcolm Pirnie, Inc., White Plains, New York
EDWIN H. CLARK II, Clean Sites, Inc., Alexandria, Virginia
ELLIS COWLING, North Carolina State University, Raleigh
GEORGE P. DASTON, The Procter & Gamble Co., Cincinnati, Ohio
PETER L. DEFUR, Virginia Commonwealth University, Richmond
DAVID L. EATON, University of Washington, Seattle
DIANA FRECKMAN, Colorado State University, Ft. Collins
ROBERT A. FROSCH, Harvard University, Cambridge, Massachusetts
DANIEL KREWSKI, Health & Welfare Canada, Ottawa, Ontario
RAYMOND C. LOEHR, The University of Texas, Austin
WARREN MUIR, Hampshire Research Institute, Alexandria, Virginia
GORDON ORIANS, University of Washington, Seattle
GEOFFREY PLACE, The Procter & Gamble, Co., (retired), South Carolina
BURTON H. SINGER, Princeton University, New Jersey
MARGARET STRAND, Bayh, Connaughton and Malone, Washington, D.C.
BAILUS WALKER, JR., Howard University, Washington, D.C.
GERALD N. WOGAN, Massachusetts Institute of Technology, Cambridge
TERRY F. YOSIE, Ruder Finn, Washington, D.C.

Staff

JAMES J. REISA, Director
DAVID J. POLICANSKY, Associate Director and Program Director for Natural Resources and Applied Ecology
CAROL A. MACZKA, Program Director for Toxicology and Risk Assessment
LEE R. PAULSON, Program Director for Information Systems and Statistics
RAYMOND A. WASSEL, Program Director for Environmental Sciences and Engineering

WATER SCIENCE AND TECHNOLOGY BOARD

DAVID L. FREYBERG, *Chair*, Stanford University, California
BRUCE E. RITTMANN, *Vice Chair*, Northwestern University, Evanston, Illinois
LINDA ABRIOLA, University of Michigan, Ann Arbor
JOHN BRISCOE, The World Bank, Washington, D.C.
WILLIAM M. EICHBAUM, The World Wildlife Fund, Washington, D.C.
WILFORD R. GARDNER, University of California, (retired), Berkeley
EVILLE GORHAM, University of Minnesota, St. Paul
THOMAS M. HELLMAN, Bristol-Myers Squibb Company, New York
CHARLES D. D. HOWARD, Charles Howard and Associates, Ltd., Victoria, British Columbia, Canada
CAROL A. JOHNSTON, University of Minnesota, Duluth
WILLIAM M. LEWIS, JR., University of Colorado, Boulder
JOHN W. MORRIS, J. W. Morris, Limited, Arlington, Virginia
CHARLES R. O'MELIA, The Johns Hopkins University, Baltimore, Maryland
REBECCA T. PARKIN, American Public Health Association, Washington, D.C.
IGNACIO RODRIGUEZ-ITURBE, Texas A&M University, College Station
FRANK W. SCHWARTZ, Ohio State University, Columbus
HENRY VAUX, JR., University of California, Riverside

Staff

STEPHEN D. PARKER, Director
SHEILA D. DAVID, Senior Staff Officer
CHRIS ELFRING, Senior Staff Officer
JACQUELINE A. MACDONALD, Senior Staff Officer
GARY D. KRAUSS, Staff Officer
ANGELA F. BRUBAKER, Research Assistant
JEANNE AQUILINO, Administrative Associate
ANITA A. HALL, Administrative Assistant
ELLEN DE GUZMAN, Senior Project Assistant
STEPHANIE VANN, Senior Project Assistant

COMMISSION ON GEOSCIENCES, ENVIRONMENT, AND RESOURCES

GEORGE M. HORNBERGER, *Chair*, University of Virginia, Charlottesville
PATRICK R. ATKINS, Aluminum Company of America, Pittsburgh, Pennsylvania
JAMES P. BRUCE, Canadian Climate Program Board, Ottawa, Ontario, Canada
WILLIAM L. FISHER, The University of Texas, Austin
JERRY F. FRANKLIN, University of Washington, Seattle
THOMAS E. GRAEDEL, Yale University, New Haven, Connecticut
DEBRA KNOPMAN, Progressive Foundation, Washington, D.C.
KAI N. LEE, Williams College, Williamstown, Massachusetts.
PERRY L. McCARTY, Stanford University, California
JUDITH E. MCDOWELL, Woods Hole Oceanographic Institution, Massachusetts
RICHARD A. MESERVE, Covington & Burling, Washington, D.C.
S. GEORGE PHILANDER, Princeton University, New Jersey
RAYMOND A. PRICE, Queen's University at Kingston, Ontario, Canada
THOMAS C. SCHELLING, University of Maryland, College Park
ELLEN SILBERGELD, University of Maryland Medical School, Baltimore
VICTORIA J. TSCHINKEL, Landers and Parsons, Tallahassee, Florida
E-AN ZEN, University of Maryland, College Park

Staff

STEPHEN RATTIEN, Executive Director
STEPHEN D. PARKER, Associate Executive Director
MORGAN GOPNIK, Assistant Executive Director
GREGORY SYMMES, Reports Officer
JAMES MALLORY, Administrative Officer
SANDI FITZPATRICK, Administrative Associate
MARQUITA SMITH, Administrative Assistant/Technology Analyst

THE NATIONAL ACADEMIES

National Academy of Sciences
National Academy of Engineering
Institute of Medicine
National Research Council

The **National Academy of Sciences** is a private, nonprofit, self-perpetuating society of distinguished scholars engaged in scientific and engineering research, dedicated to the furtherance of science and technology and to their use for the general welfare. Upon the authority of the charter granted to it by the Congress in 1863, the Academy has a mandate that requires it to advise the federal government on scientific and technical matters. Dr. Bruce M. Alberts is president of the National Academy of Sciences.

The **National Academy of Engineering** was established in 1964, under the charter of the National Academy of Sciences, as a parallel organization of outstanding engineers. It is autonomous in its administration and in the selection of its members, sharing with the National Academy of Sciences the responsibility for advising the federal government. The National Academy of Engineering also sponsors engineering programs aimed at meeting national needs, encourages education and research, and recognizes the superior achievements of engineers. Dr. Wm. A. Wulf is president of the National Academy of Engineering.

The **Institute of Medicine** was established in 1970 by the National Academy of Sciences to secure the services of eminent members of appropriate professions in the examination of policy matters pertaining to the health of the public. The Institute acts under the responsibility given to the National Academy of Sciences by its congressional charter to be an adviser to the federal government and, upon its own initiative, to identify issues of medical care, research, and education. Dr. Harvey V. Fineberg is president of the Institutedicine.

The **National Research Council** was organized by the National Academy of Sciences in 1916 to associate the broad community of science and technology with the Academy's purposes of furthering knowledge and advising the federal government. Functioning in accordance with general policies determined by the Academy, the Council has become the principal operating agency of both the National Academy of Sciences and the National Academy of Engineering in providing services to the government, the public, and the scientific and engineering communities. The Council is administered jointly by both Academies and the Institute of Medicine. Dr. Bruce M. Alberts and Dr. Wm. A. Wulf are chair and vice chair, respectively, of the National Research Council.

www.national-academies.org

Preface

As we approach the twenty-first century, the task of protecting human health and the environment is becoming ever more complex. Growing worldwide population, industrial growth, and related pressures on the environment, combined with a realization of the tremendous complexity of environmental systems, present us with new challenges. Identification of possible environmental problems early in their evolution, continued development of knowledge needed to better understand the severity and impact of these problems, and implementation of appropriate steps based on sound science to avoid or prevent the important problems and greatest risks are essential for the stewardship of the planet. The U.S. Environmental Protection Agency (EPA), as the lead environmental protection agency in the United States, must have the scientific capacity to address both current and future environmental problems. To maintain and enhance this capacity, the EPA, in addition to carrying out its mandate to implement environmental laws, must maintain a strong research program.

In the fall of 1995, the EPA Office of Research and Development (ORD) requested that the National Research Council (NRC) advise the agency on research opportunities and priorities that could help EPA address current and future environmental problems. To accomplish this task, the NRC, through its Board on Environmental Studies and Toxicology and its Water Science and Technology Board, established a multidisciplinary committee, the Committee on Research Opportunities and Priorities for EPA (See Appendix 3 for biographical sketches of committee members.). The committee's members collectively possess decades of experience in governmental and nongovernmental organizations working on research and solutions related to important environmental problems. The NRC committee gathered relevant information for this report by meeting with and interviewing individuals from many organizations and with diverse backgrounds and by reviewing previous reports that have addressed similar topics. In addition, the committee drew upon the broad knowledge and experience of its members.

This report is intended to help shape a new framework for research conducted and sponsored by EPA. As such it does not contain a detailed assessment of current activities, management policies, or budgets. Nor does it provide prescriptive guidance in respect to implementation of its recommendations. Rather, it is a broad, forward-looking document intended to assist EPA managers responsible for strategic planning for the Office of Research and Development in laying out new directions and policies for the Agency. It should also be of value to Congress and the White House as they consider appropriate roles and directions for EPA.

Another NRC committee, the Committee on Research and Peer Review at EPA, has been working in parallel with this committee. That committee, whose report will be released later in 1997, is exploring questions concerning EPA's research management practices. Its findings should serve as a useful complement to the research framework presented in this report.

The committee hopes that this report will help EPA and the nation add to the building blocks of scientific knowledge needed to better protect human health and the environment. Our aim is to ensure that the EPA develops a permanent mechanism for conducting the research necessary for better environmental stewardship. At the same time, the EPA must work cooperatively with others to take advantage of important research being carried out in other organizations.

Because EPA's mandate is so broad, and its research correspondingly wide-ranging, no single discipline or research topic could be covered fully in this report. The many shaded boxes serve as illustrative examples of valuable research areas. Many other important topics could also serve to illustrate the themes laid out in this document.

The ideas presented in this report represent the breadth of knowledge and creativity of the committee members. Committee discussions were wide-ranging and thought provoking. It was a pleasure serving as chair and being a member of such a capable, hard-working, and distinguished group of individuals.

The committee is very grateful for the assistance and dedication of the NRC staff who aided the committee and helped prepare this report. In particular, we wish to recognize Morgan Gopnik, study director, whose expertise added to the discussions and whose hard work and skill in organizing, integrating, and polishing the various chapters are responsible for the readability of the report. In addition, we would like to recognize and thank Sheila David for her hard work and assistance in helping prepare and finalize the committee report. In addition, we would like to thank Adrienne Davis for arranging the committee's meetings and to thank Stephanie Vann for bringing the manuscript to completion. Finally, we wish to recognize the staff members of EPA's ORD for their dialogues with the committee and for their continued efforts to manage a high-quality research program in the face of difficult budget constraints.

RAYMOND C. LOEHR
Chair

Contents

	EXECUTIVE SUMMARY	1
1	ENVIRONMENTAL CHALLENGES	5
	Solving Problems	5
	Recognizing Limitations	6
	Complexity, Unpredictability, and Surprise	9
	EPA's Research Challenge	10
	History and Purpose of This Study	11
	Scope of This Report	12
2	IMPROVING OUR UNDERSTANDING OF ENVIRONMENTAL ISSUES	13
	Identifying Current and Emerging Problems	13
	A Framework for Environmental Research	16
	Core Research	17
	Implementing a Core Research Program	32
3	ACHIEVING A FOCUSED RESEARCH AGENDA	37
	Anticipating Emerging Environmental Problems	37
	Identifying Environmental Problems in Need of Focused Attention	41
	Criteria for Prioritizing Among Identified Issues	43
	Developing and Maintaining Risk Assessment Capabilities at EPA	47
	Retaining Flexibility	48
4	EPA'S POSITION IN THE BROADER ENVIRONMENTAL RESEARCH ENTERPRISE	49
	EPA's Role in Research	49
	Partnerships with Other Government Organizations and the Private Sector	49

	Strengthening Scientific Capacity at EPA	53
	Improving Cooperative Data Collection and Evaluation	55
5	SUMMARY, CONCLUSIONS, AND RECOMMENDATIONS	59
	Summary	59
	Conclusions	59
	Recommendations	62
	REFERENCES	67
	APPENDIXES	
1	INTERIM REPORT OF THE COMMITTEE ON RESEARCH OPPORTUNITIES AND PRIORITIES FOR EPA	73
2	REPORTS ANALYZED TO IDENTIFY PRIORITY ENVIRONMENTAL ISSUES	81
3	BIOGRAPHICAL SKETCHES OF COMMITTEE MEMBERS	83

List of Boxes, Figures, and Tables

BOXES

1-1	Selenium Contamination at Kesterson National Wildlife Refuge: Research Helps Solve Identified Environmental Problem	7
2-1	The Three Components of Core Environmental Research	18
2-2	Soil and Ground Water Contamination: Limited Knowledge of Environmental processes Slowed Progress	20
2-3	Understanding Humic Substances: Core Research Can Be Used to Address a Variety of Environmental Problems	21
2-4	The Impact of Airborne Particulates on Human Health: Core Research Needed to Identify Cause-and-Effect Relationships	22
2-5	Measuring Large-Scale Air Pollution: Application of New Tools	24
2-6	Applying Biological Microchip Technology to Environmental Assessment, Analysis, and Remediation Problems	26
2-7	Sub-Microgram Analysis Techniques for Geochemical and Geophysical Characterization	27
2-8	Human Variability in Toxic Response: Incomplete Understanding of Biological Processes Hinders Accurate Risk Assessments	28
2-9	Risk Characterization and Communication: Developing Better Methods to Apply to Many Environmental Problems	30
2-10	The Challenges of Long-Term Ecosystem Monitoring	34
3-1	Nutrient Contamination of Coastal Waters: Attacking a Difficult Problem	38
3-2	Effectiveness of Control Strategies for Tropospheric Ozone	42
3-3	Drinking Water Disinfection	44
3-4	Criteria for Selecting Among Identified Environmental Issues	45
3-5	Environmental Endocrine Modulators: Reducing Uncertainties	47

4-1	Global Climate Change: A Large-Scale, Complex Problem Requires an Interdisciplinary, Multi-Agency Approach	51
4-2	Long-Term Studies Lead to Understanding of Complex Interactions	56

FIGURES

1-1	Chlorofluorocarbons (CFCs) and ozone depletion: Advances in science and policy through 1996	8
2-1	Accurate, sustained monitoring efforts at the Mauna Loa Observatory in Hawaii demonstrated rising levels of carbon dioxide in the atmosphere— an important piece of the climate change puzzle	31
2-2	Elements of a successful environmental monitoring program	32
3-1	Identification and mitigation of environmental problems is a continual process	39
3-2	The growth of industry and agriculture in the past 200 years has promoted at least six identifiable components of global environmental change	40
3-3	The risk assessment process	46
4-1	Some of the many partners in the environmental research endeavor	50
5-1	A framework for environmental research at EPA	61

TABLES

2-1	Identified Environmental Issues	14
2-2	Key Processes Underlying Environmental Systems	19
2-3	Environmental Research and Management Tools	25
5-1	Recommended Actions for EPA	64

BUILDING A FOUNDATION FOR SOUND ENVIRONMENTAL DECISIONS

Executive Summary

In order to provide the knowledge needed to solve environmental problems, the U.S. Environmental Protection Agency (EPA) must continue to support and maintain a strong research effort. An evolving understanding of the complexity, magnitude, and inter-relatedness of environmental problems leads us to conclude that a new balance of research programs will be helpful in achieving this goal.

The charge to this committee was to provide an overview of significant emerging environmental issues; identify and prioritize research themes and projects that are most relevant to understanding and resolving these issues; and consider the role of EPA's research program in addressing these issues in the context of research being conducted or sponsored by other organizations. After careful deliberation, the committee decided to go beyond simply presenting a limited list of important issues. Such an exercise would provide a mere snapshot in time, based on the insights of one particular collection of individuals. Instead, this report provides a broad overview of many important current and emerging environmental issues. It then presents a useful framework for thinking about and planning environmental research and describes major research themes and programs of relevance to EPA. (This committee was not asked to, and did not, address issues concerning EPA's research infrastructure, the appropriate balance between internal and external research, or appropriate mechanisms for peer review. A second NRC committee is examining these sorts of questions. Its report will be available later in 1997.)

This report defines two kinds of environmental research—*problem-driven research* and *core research*. Problem-driven research is targeted at understanding and solving particular, identified environmental problems. Core research aims to provide broader, more generic information that will help improve understanding of many problems now and in the future. Core research includes three components:

(1) acquisition of a more systematic understanding of the physical, chemical, biological, geological, social, and economic processes that underlie environmental systems at various spatial and temporal scales, and the biochemical and physiological processes in humans that are affected by environmental agents;

(2) development of broadly applicable research tools, including better techniques for measuring variables of interest (including both structural and functional attributes), more accurate models of complex systems and their interactions, and new methods for analyzing, displaying, and using environmental information in science-based decision making; and

(3) design, implementation, and maintenance of appropriate environmental monitoring programs, with evaluation, analysis, synthesis, and dissemination of the data and results. These monitoring programs are essential for understanding the status of, and changes to, environmental resources over time, and for conducting retrospective evaluations of the costs and benefits of environmental policies. Retrospective evaluations are critical to ensuring that environmental policies are achieving their intended goals at a reasonable cost without creating unpredicted, undesirable side-effects.

EPA should establish an approximately even balance between problem-driven and core research. The distinction between core and problem-driven research is not always clear-cut. Research programs can have multiple goals and motivations. Yet history, experience, and political realities indicate that there is value in defining and re-emphasizing the importance of core research at EPA. (Specific examples that illustrate how a more comprehensive core research agenda would assist in understanding environmental issues are presented in shaded boxes throughout the report.)

Because the task of protecting the environment and minimizing environmentally-related human health impacts is so vast and available resources are so limited, this report suggests criteria that can be used to identify and prioritize among important research areas. The approaches for making these choices will be different in the core and problem-driven portions of the research program. Core research should seek better understanding of fundamental phenomena and generate broadly applicable research tools and information. These goals will not vary much over time and thus core research priorities will stay relatively constant. Choices between research areas should be made based on their broad relevance to EPA's mission and on scientific merit. Cross-cutting, interdisciplinary studies that draw on findings from different fields will be of particular value. After broad program areas are selected, a key criterion for selecting core research projects is the quality of the proposed science and the ability of the investigators, as determined by a peer-review process.

Problem-driven research will be more responsive to regulatory activities and other immediate needs and should be targeted at maximizing reduction of risks. Evaluation of problem-driven research areas should focus on the risks and uncertainties associated with each problem. Although risk assessment and management provide a good framework for choosing among issues, the methodology must be refined to achieve more accurate assessments. Problem-driven research should be re-evaluated and refocused on a regular basis to ensure that the most pressing problems are being addressed. Unlike core research priorities that may not change much over time, for problem-driven research EPA must develop adaptive feedback capabilities to allow the agency to change directions when new issues arise and old issues are "solved" or judged to pose less risk than expected. A thorough identification of environmental and human health issues is the necessary first step in selecting the right issues for attention. For this reason, a continuous, internal mechanism for identifying current and emerging environmental issues from a wide range of sources, including an analysis of the implications of the latest core research findings, is critical to EPA's research endeavor.

With its limited budget and staff, and broad mandate, it is not possible or reasonable for EPA to act alone in understanding and addressing all environmental problems. Many other federal agencies, state agencies, academic institutions, and private companies have played and will continue to play important roles in environmental research. Cooperation with others will be particularly needed in the areas of human health assessment, environmental monitoring (a complex and costly undertaking), and in the investigation of global-scale issues. In order to facilitate cooperation with others and improve internal planning EPA should compile, publish, and disseminate an annual summary of all research being conducted or funded by the agency.

Good science is essential for sound environmental decision-making. By implementing the recommendations contained in this report, EPA can increase the effectiveness of its research program and thus continue to play an important role in efforts to protect the environment and human health into the next century.

1
Environmental Challenges

SOLVING PROBLEMS

Since environmental issues first engaged the public's interest, our nation's approach to environmental protection has been geared towards remediating specific, identified problems. These problems typically have gained attention due either to impacts on affected communities or to predictions from scientists and others of the likely effects of certain environmental stresses before these effects were widely recognized. Early examples of such problems included fish kills in contaminated surface waters, smog hazes over many American cities, the effects of DDT and other pesticides on wildlife, the effects of acid rain on ecosystems, the effects of lead on infants and children, and the effects of tributyl tin (a marine antifouling compound) on marine ecosystems.

When the public has perceived an environmental or public health threat as posing a serious risk, widespread concern has often led to the passage of legislation designed to reduce that threat. Examples of such legislation include the Clean Air Act, Clean Water Act, Safe Drinking Water Act, Toxic Substances Control Act, Resource Conservation and Recovery Act, and Comprehensive Environmental Response, Compensation, and Liability Act (also known as Superfund). The U.S. Environmental Protection Agency (EPA), created in 1970 with the broad mission of protecting human health and the environment, has the pressing and continuing task of implementing such laws: media- and substance-specific programs were created to develop appropriate regulations, and EPA's Office of Research and Development was asked to support this regulatory process by providing scientific expertise and research support.

The strategy of responding to recognized environmental issues has been effective in many cases. (Note that throughout this report we define "environmental issues" to include any issue affecting human health, ecosystems, natural resources, or the global environment.) The average level of lead in children's blood declined by 75% between 1978 and 1995 due to bans on the use of leaded gasoline and lead-based paint; fish have returned to rivers and lakes once considered "dead"; the air in many cities is clearer than it was 30 years ago; and the production of ozone-destroying chemicals has been reduced drastically (EPA, 1995). Environmental research played an important part in these successes, as illustrated by the example of the restoration of the Kesterson National Wildlife Refuge in Box 1-1. However, a problem-oriented approach also has limitations that are increasingly apparent.

RECOGNIZING LIMITATIONS

It has become increasingly evident that environmental systems are complex and interconnected. In looking back at early environmental successes it appears that, in many cases, attempts to correct one environmental problem unwittingly created or exacerbated others. The interplay of atmospheric particulates and sulfur oxides provides one example.

Acid deposition in the northeastern United States increased substantially over the same time period in which EPA regulations reduced powerplant emissions of particles larger than 2mm by 78% (EPA, 1996). Although the removal of larger particulates from atmospheric emissions resulted in substantially clearer urban air, the bulk of those particulates were alkaline and tended to neutralize the acidic sulfur oxides. To remedy the ecosystem and health effects associated with acidic aerosols, the sulfur in atmospheric emissions needs to be removed. But the removal of sulfur seems to lead to another unanticipated effect. Very small sulfuric acid aerosols also serve as nuclei for the formation of clouds—the more nuclei, the more small cloud droplets will be present. These droplets scatter incoming solar radiation before it reaches the earth's surface, resulting in a global cooling effect that partially offsets the warming effect of greenhouse gas buildup. A decrease in sulfuric acid in the atmosphere, aimed at reducing acid deposition and its harmful effects, may affect this global heat balance with unknown consequences (NRC, 1996b).

Another example of the complexity of environmental interactions is shown in Figure 1-1. The widespread use of chlorofluorocarbons (CFCs) as apparently safe, inert refrigerants and propellants led to depletion of the earth's protective ozone layer. CFC use provided a safer home environment but led to a serious global environmental problem.

Still another example of the interconnectedness of environmental problems is the rapid invasion of the non-native zebra mussel into Lake Erie, which has caused fouling of structures such as water intakes, outfall pipes, and piers. Engineers have experienced some success in designing materials that resist mussel colonization. However, this solution will not help remedy another, more surprising problem: it appears that the mussels are increasing the concentration of chemical contaminants throughout the aquatic food web in the lake and adjacent rivers.

> **BOX 1-1 SELENIUM CONTAMINATION AT KESTERSON NATIONAL WILDLIFE REFUGE: RESEARCH HELPS SOLVE IDENTIFIED ENVIRONMENTAL PROBLEM**
>
> Selenium contamination at Kesterson National Wildlife Refuge in California's San Joaquin Valley drew national attention in the early 1980s. In 1982 scientists began to notice biological changes—dying cattails, algal blooms, declining use by waterfowl—in reservoir ponds, which in addition to providing wetland habitat served as irrigation drainage ponds. Further investigation revealed high levels of selenium in mosquito fish and dead and deformed bird embryos. While the California Department of Public Health issued notices limiting waterfowl consumption from the Kesterson area and the U.S. Fish and Wildlife Service closed the ponds to public access, it was broad, ongoing research on the underlying geochemical, material transport, and hydrologic processes in the area that revealed the source and potential scope of the problem and provided managers with the necessary information to begin to look for solutions (NRC, 1989).
>
> Investigations found that the soils on the west side of the San Joaquin Valley are derived primarily from marine sedimentary rock containing high levels of soluble salts and pyritic materials. Selenium and seleniferous salts are commonly associated with pyritic material. Thus, as irrigation water, applied to cropland, percolated through the soil, it leached out the selenium. This selenium-laden water was then transported though a system of drainage canals to the closed basin ponds at Kesterson. With no outlet, the selenium was concentrated by evaporation to toxic levels and accumulated in the biota. Research also found that the pH and redox conditions of the system can affect selenium toxicity.
>
> While the Bureau of Reclamation, which is responsible for federal irrigation projects in the West, anticipated problems associated with the management of saline soils and drainage water in the San Joaquin Valley and had made plans to mitigate them, it did not anticipate selenium contamination. As a result of breakthroughs in selenium research, the Bureau has since been able to assess the potential for selenium contamination at other federal irrigation projects. Research on selenium speciation continues, creating the knowledge that will be needed to continue to address selenium contamination problems.

Due to past industrial practices, significant amounts of persistent, toxic compounds are buried in sediments at the bottom of Lake Erie. The mussels consume and recirculate these contaminated sediments, re-introducing them into the rest of the food chain. Thus, one environmental problem, the physical manifestation of this introduced species, turns out to be linked to a seemingly unrelated environmental

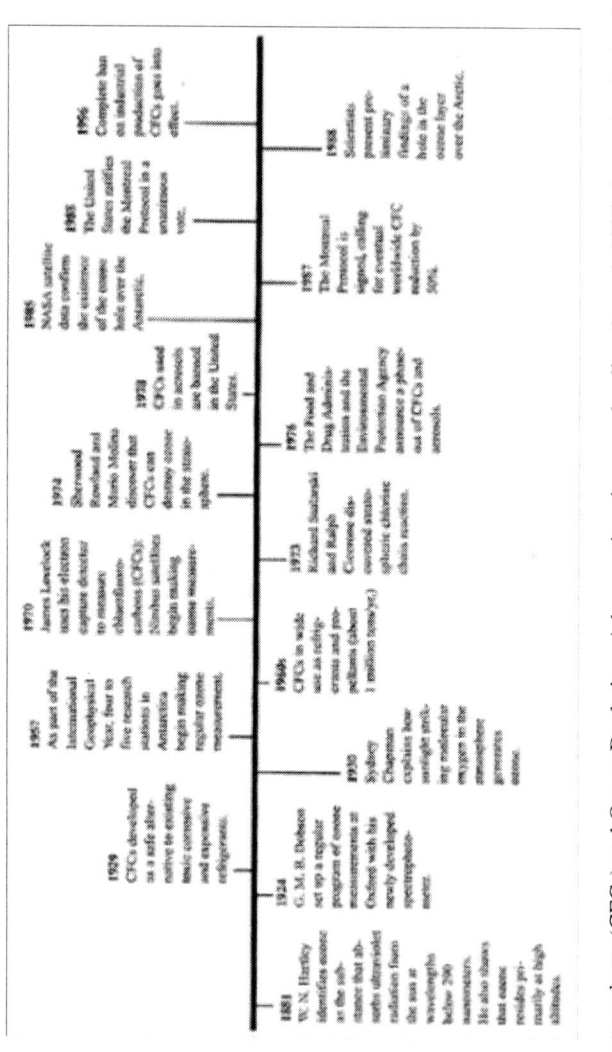

FIGURE 1-1 Chlorofluorocarbons (CFCs) and Ozone Depletion: Advances in science and policy through 1996. A growing body of chemical and atmospheric research led to the prediction of a potential problem that was then detected at an early stage. If the problem had not been recognized and addressed until the effects of increased UVB (such as skin cancer, ecosystem damage, etc.) were discernable, ecosystem and human health impacts would have been more severe, and effective mitigation would have been extremely difficult. SOURCE: Adapted from *The Ozone Depletion Phenomenon* (NAS, 1996).

problem, chemical contamination of aquatic ecosystems. Many actions that would be adequate to solve the first problem could be ineffective in solving the second.

Other examples can be cited where efforts to solve a specific problem must be considered within a broader context. This is particularly true of the growing number of regional- and global-scale problems associated with population growth, industrial development, and the corresponding pressure on limited natural resources. Indeed, the very nature of what are recognized as "environmental" problems is changing. Recently recognized problems such as global climate change, stratospheric ozone depletion, the loss of biological diversity, long-range transport of pollutants in air or water, global pressures on ocean resources, including fish, and regional water scarcity are broader, more complex environmental problems than those that received major attention several decades ago. One of the "greenhouse gases" associated with possible climate change is carbon dioxide, once considered a harmless product of combustion. Addressing such problems in politically, socially, and economically acceptable ways will require a much greater understanding of environmental systems, including the impact of human behavior on the environment, than is currently available.

COMPLEXITY, UNPREDICTABILITY, AND SURPRISE

Our society is frequently dealing with environmental problems that have not been experience before this century. Why have complete solutions to these problems proven elusive? A hint can be found by considering three features common to environmental problems: (1) they are systems problems, with multiple causes and effects; (2) they are characterized by nonlinear relationships, including complex feedback loops; (3) they often result when incremental changes, occurring over years or decades, accumulate, causing precipitous changes in environmental variables that "directly affect the health of people, productivity of renewable resources, and vitality of societies" (Holling, 1995). Based on his analysis, Holling concludes that environmental problems are "not amenable to solutions based on knowledge of small parts of the whole or on assumptions of constancy or stability of fundamental relationships."

Because of the complexity of natural systems, the inherent uncertainty in measurements, as well as the synergies and amplification effects that can occur, environmental problems will often include a strong element of surprise. At least three types of environmental surprises can be distinguished: (1) events with predictable consequences whose timing and magnitude are unexpected, such as the Exxon Valdez oil spill or the Chernobyl nuclear accident; (2) discontinuities in seemingly smooth trends, such as the sudden drop in pH that occurs when the buffering capacity of a water body is exceeded; and (3) unanticipated consequences of deliberate actions, such as the effects of using leaded gasoline on health or the relationship between widespread CFC use and stratospheric ozone depletion. As Kates and Clark (1996) conclude, "The next 25 years will surely bring more surprises. The occurrence of such surprises, of course, will not be new. What will be new is the rapidity with which they emerge, the complexity of their sources and consequences, and the difficulty we will experience in devising appropriate institutional responses."

The seeds of future surprises often lie in our response to current surprises. For example, in response to the now-recognized deleterious effect of CFCs on stratospheric ozone, industries are seeking to replace them with safer substitutes. Trifluoroacetic acid (TFA) is a breakdown product of several CFC replacements. Although TFA appears to be harmless in the atmosphere, its potential for accumulation in terrestrial and aquatic ecosystems is only now being assessed. If TFA does accumulate, it may contain the makings of a future surprise.

Unanticipated environmental problems, "surprises," are an inevitable consequence of the complexity of environmental systems and expanding human activity. By expanding our understanding of environmental systems, we will be more likely to understand the consequences of particular actions, thus avoiding some surprises, and be better prepared to respond to the inevitable surprises that will arise.

EPA'S RESEARCH CHALLENGE

Because EPA is a regulatory agency, questions have long arisen about the role EPA should play in sponsoring and conducting environmental research. Yet, to be an effective regulator, EPA must understand underlying environmental processes. To paraphrase Vannevar Bush (1945), an agency that depends exclusively on others for its basic scientific and technical knowledge will be slow in its progress and weak in its attempts to protect human health and the environment.

EPA's research program has been expected to support the immense and widely varied array of regulatory and enforcement activities within the agency, providing the scientific and technological bases for decisions. Not surprisingly, the problem-by-problem approach to environmental protection has also influenced the nature of environmental research at EPA.

Clearly, EPA cannot conduct or sponsor research on every issue of concern to the public, the Congress, or even its own program offices. At just over $500 million a year, the environmental research budget at EPA is small compared to the breadth and complexity of the issues it confronts and small even as a fraction of our nation's environmental research portfolio. In 1995, EPA's research budget accounted for only 8% of total annual environmental research expenditures by federal agencies (Teich, 1996). Hence, environmental research topics at EPA must be chosen carefully, in the context of broader national and international efforts, and efforts must be made to link EPA to these other sources of information.

Acting on recommendations from a variety of expert review committees (Carnegie Commission, 1992; EPA/SAB, 1988, 1990, 1994; EPA, 1992; MITRE,

1994; NAPA, 1994, 1995; NRC, 1993a, 1995b), EPA's Office of Research and Development (ORD) set out in 1995 to create a new mission statement, strategic plan, and organizational structure to help focus and prioritize the many demands on its limited resources. The strategic plan (EPA, 1996) is based on risk assessment concepts and calls for EPA to:

- focus research and development on the greatest risks to people and the environment, taking into account their potential severity, magnitude, and uncertainty; and
- focus research on reducing uncertainty in risk assessment and on cost-effective approaches for preventing and managing risks (EPA, 1996).

As concluded in the interim report of this committee (Appendix 1), risk assessment is one useful tool for organizing research, but it has limitations. Not all environmental issues can be assessed and ranked within the risk paradigm. The more complex and global the problem, the more difficult the task of risk assessment will be. While the risk-based research strategy is sound, it must be augmented and adapted to encompass potential and emerging risks as well as current ones. (A more detailed discussion of the appropriate role for, and limitations of, risk assessment is presented in Chapters 2 and 3.)

ORD's strategic plan also sets a goal of working with others to identify, characterize, and resolve "emerging" environmental issues. The work of this committee is intended to help EPA in this ongoing effort to define its research agenda.

HISTORY AND PURPOSE OF THIS STUDY

In the fall of 1995, EPA's assistant administrator for research and development, Dr. Robert Huggett, asked the National Research Council (NRC) to undertake a study of research opportunities and priorities for EPA. In response, the NRC, through its Board on Environmental Studies and Toxicology and its Water Science and Technology Board, established a multidisciplinary committee (see Appendix 3 for biographical sketches of committee members). The committee was charged with the following tasks:

- provide an overview of significant emerging environmental issues;
- identify and prioritize research themes and projects that are most relevant to understanding and resolving these issues; and
- consider the role of EPA's research program in addressing these issues, in the context of research being conducted or sponsored by other organizations.

The charge did not include a review of existing research programs at EPA or elsewhere, nor an assessment of issues related to organization and management of EPA's research program. (A companion NRC study, initiated shortly before this one, is currently examining research management practices at EPA. The report of that study, *Improving Research Management and Peer Review Practices in the U.S. Environmental Protection Agency,* will be available by the fall of 1997.) An interim report from this committee (Appendix 1) assessed the ORD draft strategic plan. This final report is based on collection of information related to environmental research programs and deliberations, including four committee meetings, over a period of approximately nine months.

SCOPE OF THIS REPORT

This report includes a broad overview of current and emerging environmental issues, as compiled from a review of two dozen recent reports on environmental research augmented by committee input. After much discussion, the committee decided that, rather than simply turn this rather long list into a shorter list of problems that appear important at this moment in time, it would be more useful to EPA to describe a lasting framework for environmental research and encourage the agency to build and nurture its own internal capacity for identifying and selecting future research areas. The report also describes major research themes and programs of relevance to EPA; suggests criteria that can be used to identify and prioritize among important research areas; recommends actions EPA should take to build its scientific capacity; and provides illustrations of the kinds of research projects that EPA should consider.

This report is not intended to be highly technical. The advice it contains is targeted primarily to an audience of environmental policymakers and managers, as well as anyone with a broad interest in the conduct of environmental research. The report explains how environmental research can play a critical role in achieving the dual goals of finding workable solutions to current environmental problems while developing the scientific capacity to recognize and better respond to future problems. As stated in the report *Safeguarding the Future: Credible Science, Credible Decisions* (EPA, 1992):

> [S]cience is one of the soundest investments the nation can make for the future. Strong science provides the foundation for credible environmental decision making. With a better understanding of environmental risks to people and ecosystems, EPA can target the hazards that pose the greatest risks, anticipate environmental problems before they reach a critical level, and develop strategies that use the nation's, and the world's, environmental protection dollars wisely.

2

Improving Our Understanding of Environmental Issues

IDENTIFYING CURRENT AND EMERGING PROBLEMS

As stated in Chapter 1, the charge for this study included the identification of significant emerging environmental issues and identification of research themes and projects most relevant to understanding and resolving these issues. In this report, environmental issues have been defined broadly to include those affecting human health, ecosystems, natural resources, or the global environment. Many individuals and expert committees over the years have addressed aspects of this charge. Thus, reviewing and summarizing their recommendations was an appropriate starting point for deliberations. Two dozen reports were reviewed and summarized, including many issued by the National Research Council and by EPA's Science Advisory Board, and others by technical societies and research institutes (see Appendix 2 for a list of these reports). Particular attention was paid to reports developed through the consensus of an expert committee. Each report was analyzed to reveal important current and emerging environmental concerns and associated research recommendations. The committee members also identified environmental issues that have stimulated their research interests and activities.

The resultant range of current and emerging environmental concerns identified in this manner is presented in Table 2-1, with the issues grouped into broad categories. This list is not intended to be comprehensive, nor are the elements entirely consistent with one another. The list is simply a summary of environmental issues indicated as being of concern by knowledgeable groups or individuals. The environmental concerns that are arrayed range from very tangible, narrowly focused, near-term environmental problems to broadly based environmental issues. It became apparent that recommendations from more recent reports tend to focus on "overarching" issues such as sustainability or risk/benefit

TABLE 2-1 Identified Environmental Issues

Clean Air
  Automotive emissions
  Industrial emissions
  Photochemical air pollution
  Acid deposition
  Airborne toxic substances
  Particulate matter
  Long-range pollutant transport
  Sudden, accidental releases of hazardous air pollutants
  Urban and regional-scale tropospheric ozone

Clean Streams, Rivers, Lakes, and Estuaries
  Industrial discharges
  Municipal waste discharges
  Acid mine drainage
  Agricultural runoff
  Urban runoff
  Atmospheric deposition
  Oil spills
  Thermal pollution
  Eutrophication
  Human-accelerated erosion and turbidity
  Biochemical oxygen demand
  Alterations due to floods
  Storm overflows
  Stream channelization consequences
  Effects of dams
  Introduced species
  Competition for water resources

Clean Coasts and Oceans
  Eutrophication
  Input from rivers and streams
  Chemical contamination of estuaries, coastal areas, and oceans
  Effects of recreational and commercial uses
  Changes in biodiversity
  Contaminated sediments

Clean Aquifers and Soils
  Superfund and other industrial waste sites
  Leaking fuel tanks
  Diffuse-source contamination
  Salt and heavy metal contamination
  Salt water inflow

Clean Drinking Water
  Drinking water pollutants
  Biological contamination
  Disinfection byproducts
  Inadequate water delivery systems
  Point-of-use treatment (home filters, etc.)
  Old lead and lead-soldered waterpipes
  Regional scarcity of potable water

Clean Dwellings and Workplaces
  Indoor air contaminants (including radon)
  Old lead-based paint
  Asbestos
  Outgassing from construction and finishing materials
  Toxic substances used in homes and workplaces

Safe Food Supply
  Pesticide residues
  Plant uptake of contaminants
  Effects of pollution on crops

Safe Disposal of Human Wastes
  Effective waste isolation/collection
  Sanitary waste disinfection
  Sludge disposal
  Wastewater reuse

Safe Disposal of Household and Industrial Waste
  Waste reduction and recycling
  Landfill technology and use
  Radioactive waste storage, treatment, and disposal
  Incineration emissions and ash
  Offshore disposal
  Industrial wastewater treatment
  Infrastructure needs

Habitat and Species Conservation
  Riparian degradation
  Tropical ecosystem degradation
  Temperate ecosystem degradation
  Polar ecosystem degradation
  Marine ecosystem degradation
  Wetlands degradation
  Endangered species
  Species extinction
  Overfishing
  Pollutant bioaccumulation/bioconcentration
  Habitat alteration, fragmentation, and destruction

Herbicide and pesticide effects
Land use changes

Environmental Restoration
Mining and extractive industry reclamation
Military base reclamation
Industrial site reclamation
Effects of engineered watersheds and modified hydrologic flow patterns
Ecological function impairment
Assessment of "restored" sites, including wetlands

Environmental Impacts on Human Health
Cancer
Birth defects
Genetic susceptibility
Endocrine modulators
Neurotoxicity
Immune dysfunction
Asthma and other respiratory dysfunction
Cardiovascular disease
Effects of multiple exposures

Overarching Issues

Long-Term Sustainability
Climate change
Human population growth
Ozone depletion
Land-use patterns
Natural resource allocation
Conservation of non-renewable resources
Long-term environmental monitoring
Economic mechanisms for environmental improvement
Industrial ecology

Assessment and Management of Risks
Risk assessment methodologies
Human exposure pathways
Ecosystem exposure pathways
Assessment of ecological risk
Toxicity and measures of effects
Effects of low-level exposures
Effects of multiple exposures and stressors
Psychology and perception of risk

NOTE: This list is a compilation of environmental problems identified as important by environmental experts—see explanation in text.

assessment, rather than the narrower pollutant- or media-specific problems that historically have framed environmental agendas.

Recognizing the wide range of issues and the limitation of financial resources, EPA's new *Strategic Plan for the Office of Research and Development* (EPA, 1996) articulates the need for a disciplined system of prioritization to identify the most significant issues for attention. This is a step in the right direction—focused research efforts, motivated by specific high-priority issues, will continue to be required for valid scientific and public policy reasons. However, an appreciation of the complexity and unpredictability of environmental systems leads us to conclude that even this approach to environmental research is limited because it misses the opportunity to use research to create scientific and technological building blocks or core research (the focus of this chapter), which can enhance our future ability to address a wide range of environmental problems. There is no question that problem-specific research has helped to alleviate particular problems, but, as discussed in Chapter 1, the attempted solutions often underestimate the complexity of environmental systems and rarely result in systematic strategies for managing and avoiding broad classes of environmental threats.

A promising approach to identify and address the important current and emerging environmental issues in the long run is to seek to understand the key processes that drive and connect environmental systems. The insights gained from such efforts may then be applied to many categories of current and future environmental issues. A framework that would promote this goal is described in this chapter.

A FRAMEWORK FOR ENVIRONMENTAL RESEARCH

To build the scientific capacity needed to address the complex, multidisciplinary problems facing us now and likely to emerge in the future, two complementary types of research are needed: "problem driven" and "core." This report defines these research categories and explains the benefits to be gained by establishing a balance between them.

As used in this report, the term **problem-driven research** refers to investigations that attempt to understand and solve an identified problem. Frequently these efforts are motivated by current or foreseen regulatory action. In contrast, the term **core research** is used here to describe investigations that seek to elucidate key physical, chemical, biological, geological, sociological, and economic processes that underlie environmental systems, thus providing the basis for responding to a wide range of environmental problems in a comprehensive way. This includes the biochemical and physiological processes in humans that can be affected by environmental agents. Two other important kinds of core research are the development of tools and collection of data required to detect and assess environmental threats, prevent or mitigate environmental harm, and determine whether environmental policies are effective.

Historically, much of the nation's environmental research, including research at EPA, has been directed at solving immediate problems. Over time, progress in solving fairly specific environmental problems will benefit enormously by recognizing that the enhancement of underlying knowledge, data, and research techniques will help to address many related problems. Many of the environmental problems included in Table 2-1 are merely symptoms of human-induced disruptions in underlying, highly complex environmental systems.

It is important to note that the concepts of problem-driven and core environmental research introduced above are *not* the same as the familiar categories of basic versus applied, fundamental versus directed, or short-term versus long-term research. It may be necessary to perform a great deal of what is usually called "basic" research in order to make progress in solving a particular problem. Similarly, certain technology development tasks—traditionally categorized as "applied" research—can have broad applicability and are therefore included in our definition of core research.

The distinction between core and problem-driven research is not always clear-cut; environmental research defies easy categorization. Research programs have multiple goals and motivations. When all goes well there are interactions and feedback loops between different projects, even in seemingly unrelated fields. For instance, advances in measurement, computation, and communication technologies, some of them developed with very specific applications in mind, have had profound impacts on the conduct and outcome of virtually all scientific activities.

Stokes (1995) addressed the lack of a clear distinction between core and problem-driven research using the work of Pasteur to illustrate how the drive toward fundamental understanding is inextricably linked with the drive to use scientific knowledge to address societal concerns. Stokes suggests that research activities occupy many dimensions in "inspiration space." A particularly relevant component of this space exists where a strong drive for fundamental understanding intersects with a strong sense of the usefulness of the anticipated results. Environmental research exhibits these characteristics.

> No, a thousand times no; there does not exist a category of science to which one can give the name applied science. There are science and the applications of science, bound together as the fruit to the tree which bears it. (Louis Pasteur, 1871)

Despite this absence of a firm demarcation between problem-driven and core research, experience, history, and political realities indicate that there is value in describing and re-emphasizing the critical role of core research in EPA's research portfolio. The remainder of this chapter expands on the definition and implementation of a strong core research program. The need for, and benefits of, problem-driven research are discussed in Chapter 3. That chapter also suggests ways to limit the number of specific issues that are pursued in order to use limited resources wisely and to ensure that the balance between problem-driven and core research can be maintained.

CORE RESEARCH

As defined above, core environmental research cuts across and helps to solve many related environmental problems. There are several components within this category: (1) the acquisition of systematic understanding of environmental processes, (2) the development of innovative research methods and tools, and (3) the collection, maintenance, and dissemination of accurate and comprehensive environmental data (see Box 2-1). All three components are necessary if environmental problem-solving is to be based on a foundation of sound science.

Understanding Underlying Processes

One component of a core research program is the systematic investigation of the physical, chemical, biological, geological, sociological, and economic processes that underlie environmental systems. Environmental systems include the atmosphere, hydrosphere, geosphere, and biosphere, and the interactions of all these with human populations. A representative list of these kinds of processes is shown in Table 2-2. This component includes studies of environmental impacts on biological systems and human health; clarification of the processes that underpin technological systems designed to prevent or mitigate environmental degradation; and sociological and economic processes that influence human behavior and thus environmental protection strategies. Such research must also examine the interactions and feedback among various physical, biological, and social processes.

BOX 2-1 THE THREE COMPONENTS OF CORE ENVIRONMENTAL RESEARCH

(1) **Understanding Underlying Processes**—investigation of the processes that drive environmental systems, including effects on human health.

(2) **Development of Tools**—development and demonstration of innovative research tools, including measurement techniques, models, and methods.

(3) **Acquisition of Data**—collection and dissemination of accurate, long-term environmental data.

We need to know a great deal more about these processes to understand how environmental problems are interrelated, how solutions for one problem may influence others, and whether proposed environmental management strategies are merely treating symptoms or are leading to sustainable solutions. For example, in order to better understand and predict the movement and fate of trace chemicals in the environment, we need to learn more about their concentrations, speciation, and reactivity in soil, water, and air (see Box 2-2). In order to protect human and ecosystem health, we need a more detailed understanding of molecular-level mechanisms, particularly with respect to chronic effects of chemicals present at low concentrations.

It is important to note that most of the processes listed in Table 2-2 do not map neatly to traditional disciplines such as chemistry, biology, or physics. The investigations needed to understand environmental processes are profoundly interdisciplinary. Developing fields such as ecotoxicology, biogeochemistry, and environmental microbiology will play important roles. Additional examples of the value of core research in understanding processes needed to solve environmental problems are given in Boxes 2-3 and 2-4.

TABLE 2-2 Key Processes Underlying Environmental Systems

Physical/Chemical Systems
Transport and cycling of matter in solid, liquid, and gas phases
Chemical and phase transformations
Energy flow and transformation
Interactions of physical/chemical processes with biological and social processes
Biological Systems
Biological production
Origins, functions, and maintenance of biological diversity
Reproduction and development
Metabolism, growth, and death
Cellular differentiation and proliferation
Immune function
Neurobiological function
Incidence and mechanisms of pathology
Growth and regulation of populations
Interactions of biological processes with physical/chemical and social processes
Social Systems
Resource utilization
Diffusion of science into policy
Individual and collective decision making
Economic, social, political, and legal structures
Human settlement and land use
Ethics and equity
Technological innovation and diffusion
Interactions of social processes with physical/chemical and biological processes.

NOTE: This list follows from further consideration of Table 2-1. That table lists a myriad of environmental issues, all of which could be better understood and addressed through greater understanding of the underlying processes presented here.

Development of Innovative Tools

To support improved efficiency and efficacy within the broad environmental science community, both inside and outside EPA, there must be a sustained investment in the development of innovative environmental research tools and techniques that capitalize on scientific and technological advances. Improved research tools are critical for reducing the large uncertainties in our understanding of environmental problems. Examples include pollutant concentration and flux measurement instrumentation (see Box 2-5), improved models of pollutant transport and transformation, methods to determine cellular and systematic responses to pollutants, more effective risk assessment methodology, ecosystem monitoring and modeling techniques, and environmental valuation techniques. Table 2-3 lists major categories of environmental research and management tools, including measurement and analytical techniques, environmental models, and research methods, that are central to the success of the environmental research effort.

BOX 2-2 SOIL AND GROUND WATER CONTAMINATION: LIMITED KNOWLEDGE OF ENVIRONMENTAL PROCESSES SLOWED PROGRESS

Soil and ground water contamination is a highly complex environmental problem facing the nation today. Although the exact number is uncertain, estimates of sites with contaminated soil or ground water range from 300,000 to 400,000. Required by law to clean up these sites, government agencies and industries are spending billions of dollars annually in remediation efforts. In the next 30 years, cleanup costs are estimated to be as high as $ 1 trillion. Yet, increasing evidence indicates that current technologies are not capable of cleaning up many sites to current health-based standards, and there is growing concern that the results of some cleanup efforts are not worth the huge investment of resources needed (NCR, 1994a).

The inability of conventional technologies, such as pump-and-treat systems, to clean up many contaminated sites reveals several areas where current knowledge of fundamental processes is limited. Contaminated sites are often extremely complex. Different soils and sediments have different chemical, physical, and microbial characteristics affecting treatment approaches. The site-specific differences and heterogeneity of each system further complicate site cleanup efforts. In addition to their physical complexities, many sites contain several types of contaminants.

An improved understanding of basic processes is needed in order to prevent contamination and develop more effective cleanup technologies. The processes in need of elucidation include the chemical behavior of contaminants and contaminant mixtures in complex soil and sediment matrices; effects of surfactants, oxidants, and other chemicals on solubilities and sorption of various contaminant species; and the role of colloids in transport and fate of contaminants. Research is also needed to better understand the biological and other processes underlying technologies such as bioremediation and phytoremediation.

To support this process research, new tools are also needed. These include methods to accurately and rapidly characterize subsurface physical, chemical, and microbial heterogeneity; methods to monitor bioavailability; better models of chemically reactive fluid flow; more sensitive and more accurate methods for measuring composition, molecular structure, surface structure and properties, and bulk physical properties, especially on microscopic and smaller scales; techniques for observing and modeling ground water flow patterns and rates of transport; detection and monitoring methods for subsurface contaminant plumes; and molecular modeling of particle surface structures and processes.

BOX 2-3 UNDERSTANDING HUMIC SUBSTANCES: CORE RESEARCH CAN BE USED TO ADDRESS A VARIETY OF ENVIRONMENTAL PROBLEMS

A class of naturally occurring organic compounds called humic substances has long been known to be capable of reacting with some contaminants, such as trace metals and pesticides. The presence of these humic substances was often used to explain observations of greater than predicted mobility of pesticides in ground water and higher concentrations of trace metals than calculated from water-rock interactions. However, the rigorous study of such phenomena was limited by insufficient knowledge of the chemistry of humic substances and a lack of analytical methods to concentrate and separate them.

Over a 20-year period, the U.S. Geological Survey (USGS) and others developed and tested techniques for the isolation and characterization of humic compounds. A major focus of the research was to find ways to sample, isolate, and characterize the complex organic substances that are created by the decay of plant materials. In the last 10 years the research has expanded to include the study of the effects and interactions of humic substances with trace metals, radionuclides, organic contaminants, carbon cycling in ecosystems, and formation of disinfection byproducts.

The methods developed as a result of core research on these complex substances have had a major impact on contaminant transport research. For example, in a joint USGS-Department of Energy (DOE) study, methods for isolating colloidal material and humic substances have been combined to characterize the chemical speciation of radionuclides in ground water and surface water at Rocky Flats, a nuclear weapons factory in Colorado. The results of this study show that the plutonium is distributed among particulate, colloidal, and dissolved humic fractions, whereas the uranium is found predominantly in the dissolved humic fraction. The DOE will use these results to develop treatment strategies for these contaminated waters.

This same body of core research is now being used to study the mercury cycle in South Florida. Mercury contamination is believed to be a cause of decline in the population of a number of endangered species in Florida. The mercury cycle, especially the methylation of mercury, is known to be highly related to the presence, type, and reactivity of organic matter present in the soil water. Experts in humic substances, mercury cycling, and microbiology are working to better understand the factors that lead to mercury's entry into the food chain. This knowledge will be used to evaluate various options for the restoration of the South Florida ecosystem.

BOX 2-4 THE IMPACT OF AIRBORNE PARTICULATES ON HUMAN HEALTH: CORE RESEARCH NEEDED TO IDENTIFY CAUSE-AND-EFFECT RELATIONSHIPS

The impact of airborne particulates on visibility and public health is a long recognized problem in the environment (e.g., NRC, 1993b; EPA, 1996). Significant human health risks can be associated with airborne particulates. A recent clinical study has demonstrated a link between the inhalation of airborne particulates and the development of asthma and recent careful analyses of health statistics, using novel epidemiological approaches, associate chronic exposures to fine particulates with significantly increased risks in premature deaths from cardiopulmonary disease and lung cancer. Yet there is very little basic understanding of the cause-and-effect relationships associated with fine aerosol particles and human health, including the effects of chemical composition and physical properties of particles and the mechanisms of interaction. We also need a better understanding of human exposure to particulates in order to support risk assessment and management efforts. Without this knowledge, it is very difficult to determine what aerosol properties are most important to monitor, what kinds of standards to set, and how to implement mitigation strategies.

To adequately assess and mitigate the impact of airborne particulates on human health, additional knowledge of several underlying processes is needed. These processes include the formation, chemical transformation, and growth of fine particulates in the atmosphere; interactions between photochemical oxidant chemistry and the composition and concentration of airborne aerosols; the physical and chemical properties of fine aerosols that affect human health; the physiological and toxicological mechanisms that cause fine airborne particles to affect human health; and the variance in susceptibility to adverse effects of airborne fine particles by different population subgroups.

Tools that must be improved to make further progress in understanding these underlying processes are (a) instrumentation technology needed for the measurement of the chemical composition and physical properties of primary and secondary atmospheric aerosols and associated precursors; (b) better mathematical modeling and diagnostic analysis techniques for integrating the chemical and physical processes affecting the formation, distribution, and disposition of aerosol particles in the environment; and (c) the development of long-term monitoring networks. It will also be necessary to develop animal models for cardiopulmonary responses to particulates, and exposure modeling practices that take into account the complex physical and chemical nature of airborne particulates.

> As with other environmental issues, the effects of fine particulates on air quality and the underlying processes leading to secondary aerosol formation are closely coupled with processes that lead to other air quality issues, such as photochemical oxidant/ozone formation. For this reason, it is important to address these issues as an integrated system when selecting appropriate research areas.

New tools can enable breakthroughs in understanding and managing a broad range of environmental concerns. The development of computer technology is well recognized to have changed how information is developed, distributed, analyzed, displayed, and maintained. In the same way, ongoing advances in electronics, electrochemical and geophysical techniques, electro-optics, biotechnology, communications, remote sensing, aeronautics, and other technologies will allow environmental research to be performed in ways that represent quantum leaps over methods used now. Furthermore, the successful management of environmental issues will require the development of a wide range of new tools, techniques, and processes designed to mitigate and/or prevent environmental damage. Additional examples of environmental research tools are described in Boxes 2-6 and 2-7.

Although this report endorses risk assessment in Chapter 3 as a reasonable approach for allocating resources among identified problems, current risk assessment techniques are far from perfect. The risk assessment paradigm was formulated with risk to the health of individuals in mind. Although controversial, toxicologists have developed a fair amount of experience in estimating, for example, the excess cancer risk that results from exposure of one species to one chemical. But ecosystem risks, risks from multiple stressors, and risks from mixtures of substances have proven much more difficult to quantify. Because of the complexity and variability of ecosystems, critical effects may be at the level of the individual, population, or community. Identical health effects on two different individuals, species, or populations will not necessarily have identical consequences (see Box 2-8). The "risk" involved in eliminating a species from an ecosystem is difficult even to define, let alone measure. Where it has been attempted (e.g., Tilman and Downing, 1994), long-term, detailed examinations of entire ecosystems have been necessary. Risk assessment will be very difficult to apply to broad, global issues such as climate change or resource exploitation.

Thus, risk assessment methods also are key tools for EPA. Current risk assessment practices include large uncertainties and often depend on unvalidated assumptions. Areas for improvement include methods to extrapolate from animal

BOX 2-5 MEASURING LARGE-SCALE AIR POLLUTION: APPLICATION OF NEW TOOLS

Atmospheric pollution problems, such as atmospheric acid generation and deposition, greenhouse gas buildup, and stratospheric ozone destruction, often occur over semi-continental to global scales. Observation of phenomena at these large spatial scales has confirmed the limitations of current air-quality monitoring efforts. Sparse distributions of fixed air-quality measurement sites under the control of either local or national governments are not sufficient to characterize air pollution problems on a global scale. In order to address these large-scale pollution issues, it has been necessary to develop mobile (usually airborne) platforms equipped with suites of automated analytical instruments capable of rapid, real-time measurements of gaseous and aerosol pollutant concentrations and fluxes (Albritton et al., 1990; Kolb, 1991).

The ability to map pollutant concentration distributions in three spatial dimensions as well as to follow their temporal evolution has provided powerful insights into the chemical and dynamic processes of large-scale air pollution problems. Mapping can also illuminate the relationship between emission sources and subsequent secondary pollutant production and dispersion. These tools will also be of use in assessing to what degree atmospheric pollution contributes to other environmental concerns, such as nutrient contamination of rivers, lakes, and coastal waters and degradation of forest ecosystems.

While most current platforms are piloted aircraft, it is anticipated that the extent of monitoring needed and the associated costs will require the use of unmanned air vehicles in the future. Requiring real-time, robotic operation, most instruments will employ physical (electro-optical, ion optical, etc.) rather than chemical measurement principles (Albritton et al., 1990; Kolb, 1991).

To date, U.S. progress in developing and deploying pollution measurement instrument suites and associated mobile measurement platforms has been led by the National Aeronautics and Space Administration (NASA), the National Oceanic and Atmospheric Administration (NOAA), the National Science Foundation (NSF), and the Department of Energy (DOE). EPA now has an opportunity to build on the work of these agencies adapting these technological advances to its own needs.

data to human risk; quantification of variability in human population responses; better exposure assessment for humans and ecosystems; and estimation of the level of risk at the reference, or "virtually safe," dose. These questions can be approached by better defining the underlying molecular, biochemical, and cellular changes that accumulate to produce a toxic response, and that should be measurable at or near the reference dose. Cancer and noncancer risk assessment approaches are vastly different, precluding any direct comparison of risks between carcinogenic and noncarcinogenic toxic responses. Methods for evaluating the cumulative risk of exposures to multiple chemicals are in need of refinement. Methods for communicating risks must also be improved (see Box 2-9).

TABLE 2-3 Environmental Research and Management Tools

Measurement techniques for chemical species concentrations and fluxes
Measurement techniques for biological species vitality and diversity
Measurement techniques for physical environmental variables
Biological markers of exposure and susceptibility
Models of complex environmental systems
Models of environmental-societal interactions
Techniques for studying whole ecosystems
Techniques for assessing public perceptions and values
Techniques for assessing molecular and cellular toxicity
Methods for predicting impacts of genetically altered organisms
Methods for extrapolating molecular and cellular toxicity to higher levels of biological organization
Methods of quantitative and comparative risk assessment
Methods of evaluating natural resources and environmental services
Methods for weighing environmental and personal risk factors
Methods for exposure assessment

Acquisition and Dissemination of Data

Another element of core research involves the development and maintenance of carefully selected, accurate, long-term environmental data sets to document environmental trends, set reference points for the success or failures of management strategies, and contribute to the continuous record of information about the status of the planet and its inhabitants. (Note that *environmental* monitoring in this context is different from *compliance* monitoring, which aims to discover specific violations and force corrective action.) The importance and scientific complexity of environmental monitoring has often been underestimated. The aim is not merely to assemble data but to design and carry out scientifically sound systems of environmental surveillance. The relatively recent development of global change science has underscored the critical importance of accurate, long-term data. For example, C. D. Keeling's measurements of carbon dioxide concentrations in the atmosphere (Figure 2-1) provided a foundation for subsequent studies of the "greenhouse effect." In addition, the U.S. Geological Survey's vast hydrologic data collection network provides a basis for studying and managing the nation's water resources.

The development of new tools has enabled breakthroughs in our monitoring

BOX 2-6 APPLYING BIOLOGICAL MICROCHIP TECHNOLOGY TO ENVIRONMENTAL ASSESSMENT, ANALYSIS, AND REMEDIATION PROBLEMS

Biological microchips, including DNA-and protein-containing microchips, constitute a promising new suite of tools for detecting environmentally relevant organisms and for identifying stresses on organisms or ecosystems. The basic principle underlying biological microchips is closely related to that of affinity chromatography. A chemical component specifically recognized by a certain protein or nucleic acid is attached to a solid matrix. This matrix is then used to purify the target molecules from a mixture. Microchips can contain many different molecules, ranging from small organic compounds to peptides and proteins, as well as oligonucleotides and nucleic acids, arranged in a high density two-dimensional array. The microchip arrays can be used to detect the presence of molecules that bind to the surface, be they proteins or nucleic acids (Ellington and Szostak, 1992; Giver et al., 1993; Symensma et al., 1996).

Biological microchips have the potential for broad applications in the assessment of ecosystem dynamics and health. In particular, it may be possible to develop microchips that can be used to assess and quantify soil-and water-borne microorganisms. Such a tool will be highly useful in improving ground water and soil cleanup technologies such as bioremediation, where the biological microchip could be used to monitor the survival and persistence of decontaminating microorganisms introduced into a contaminated site, as well as identify microorganisms recovered from highly contaminated sites that might be useful in bioremediation. The rapid expansion of nucleic acid sequence databases, as well as increasing knowledge of stress physiology in both plants and animals, will make it possible to develop diagnostic microchips that can monitor the stress levels in representative species within unmanaged and lightly managed ecosystems, as well as agroecosystems and urban ecosystems. Since both plants and animals respond to environmental stresses by changing the expression levels of certain genes, identification of certain stress-sensitive genes will permit the design of simple methods of assessing stress in some species. Although much of microchip-based detection technology is in its infancy, it holds great promise for providing powerful and inexpensive tools both for the detection of undesirable organisms and for assessing biodiversity and detecting stress in diverse ecosystems.

capability. Improvements in remote sensing technologies (ground-based, airborne, and satellite platforms) and development of more effective monitoring instruments (fixed-site and mobile monitors, coupled with modern communication and computer links) hold significant promise that more capable monitoring systems can be developed, deployed, and maintained. The data from these sys

> **BOX 2-7 SUB-MICROGRAM ANALYSIS TECHNIQUES FOR GEOCHEMICAL AND GEOPHYSICAL CHARACTERIZATION**
>
> Environmental research increasingly requires the ability to detect and analyze extremely small quantities of pollutants in very dilute solutions and mixtures. Recent improvements in mass spectrometry, especially the use of particle accelerators as ion sources, have made possible the detection of some elements and isotopes at sensitivities as great as 1 part in 10^{15} (Elmore and Phillips, 1987). This capability has opened up many new opportunities for understanding environmental processes. For example, the "age" of ground water samples can now be measured by analyzing their contents for cosmic-ray-produced isotopes of chlorine or bomb-produced tritium (Liu et al., 1995). Hydrologic flow regimes can be mapped and sources of river water determined using either dilute natural water constituents or introduced substances as geochemical tracers (Andersson et al., 1994). Improved sensitivity and accuracy also permit analyses of very small water, soil, or sediment samples, thus greatly reducing sampling problems and expense.
>
> In addition to having the ability to measure the presence and amount of very small quantities of a substance, it is often important to know the physical distribution of the substance on a very small scale. Contaminants frequently attach themselves to the surfaces of soil or sediment particles, react with them, or diffuse into them. Strategies for removal or isolation of the contaminants may hinge on a detailed knowledge of this sorption behavior at a microscopic or even atomic level. A variety of instruments to obtain such information is now available to environmental scientists; new instruments include electron microprobes, scanning and transmission electron microscopes, atomic force microscopes, and sensitive, high-resolution ion microprobes.

tems must be both accurate and of sufficient spatial and temporal extent to characterize large-scale and persistent environmental issues adequately. Complex environmental systems can be characterized based on either their structure or their function. Data related to both kinds of characteristics are needed to describe and understand ecosystems.

The collection of human health and socioeconomic data poses special challenges. Currently available data originate from many sources outside the environmental research community, and the data themselves are influenced by complex, interacting forces. Socioeconomic data often have been collected for purposes unrelated to the environment and are therefore not always suitable for EPA's purposes. Nevertheless, experience with the population surveys conducted by the National Center for Health Statistics shows that good coordination and

BOX 2-8 HUMAN VARIABILITY IN TOXIC RESPONSE: INCOMPLETE UNDERSTANDING OF BIOLOGICAL PROCESSES HINDERS ACCURATE RISK ASSESSMENTS

Human health risk assessment involves assumptions about the range of variability of response to toxic agents. Usually there are no data on human variability in toxic response to regulated chemicals, and a one-size-fits-all default value is used instead. Variability arises from genetics, sex, age, and health status. The range of susceptibility is one of the factors considered within the human population so that the most susceptible people will be protected. Although this consideration of variability is standard practice in risk assessment, there are virtually no data on the magnitude of that variability for any given toxicant. In the absence of information, the EPA uses a default value of 10; i.e., the range of variability between the most susceptible individual and the median is an order of magnitude. Given that the issue of variability is ubiquitous in human health risk assessment, it is of considerable public health importance that the magnitude of variability in toxic response be quantified.

Addressing the uncertainties in estimates of human variability in toxic response would improve the accuracy of risk assessment and improve EPA's ability to protect public health.

The types of information that should be obtained include

(1) Genetic basis of susceptibility: While genes that are capable of causing disease states by themselves are relatively rare (presumably through selective pressure), it has become clear recently that genes that slightly increase an individual's susceptibility to particular diseases may be common. There are a number of examples of genetic variability influencing the metabolism of, or response to, foreign substances. These genetic variations significantly affect susceptibility to particular toxic agents. For example, recent studies indicate that a common variant in the gene for the growth factor TGF-alpha may contribute to the occurrence of certain birth defects (Hwang et al., 1995). The identification of these genes, measurement of their prevalence in the population, and estimates of the increase in risk that they confer for exposure to specific agents is an important area for research in the next decade.

(2) Life-stage differences in susceptibility: While there are widely held beliefs that at certain life stages, especially childhood and old age, people may be more susceptible to toxicants, the database to support this belief is far from comprehensive, and the biological basis is not always obvious. There is considerable merit in better characterizing both the intrinsic (e.g., qualitative and quantitative differences in pharmaco-dynamics, metabolism, etc.) and extrinsic (e.g., greater exposure due to greater

> ingestion of certain foodstuffs, behavioral peculiarities) factors that contribute to life-style-related differences in susceptibility.
> (3) interaction of toxicants with pre-existing disease states: Pre-existing disorders may be a major factor in determining susceptibility but are not often characterized.
>
> Finding answers to these questions will depend to some extent on expertise such as clinical medicine and epidemiology, that is not well represented within EPA. EPA may decide to strengthen these areas or to establish formal collaborations with other federal agencies such as the National Institute of Environmental Health Sciences (NIEHS), the National Cancer Institute (NCI), or the Center for Disease Control (CDC), which may be more capable of making immediate progress in these areas.

EPA participation in the early planning stages of such data collection efforts affords optimal use of the resulting data sets by EPA. These surveys have proven to be valuable resources for studies on the health effects of lead, ozone, and particulates. (Schwartz, 1989; Schwartz and Otto, 1987).

Another source that has not been sufficiently well tapped for research purposes is the abundant data associated with regulatory compliance monitoring. Here again, the key to making these data more useful for a broad range of research endeavors is to have scientists who may use the data be involved in the planning and design of compliance monitoring programs. This dual use of data has received greater attention in other fields. For example, geophysicists have been intimately involved in the design of the global seismic network, whose primary function is to monitor compliance with the Comprehensive Test Ban Treaty.

Samples of water, soil, air, plants, and other biological materials also can be collected and archived. This would enable analyses to be conducted in the future when analytical techniques or process understanding have improved. The cost and difficulties involved in collecting and storing sufficient samples currently make this concept impractical except in specific cases. For example, taxonomists have traditionally preserved individual plant and animal specimens for the purpose of identification and classification (NRC, 1995d). To the degree this is done, it might be conducted in coordination with the U.S. Geological Survey's Biological Resources Division.

Of course, mere collection of environmental data or samples is not sufficient in itself. The information must be reduced, evaluated, and maintained in an accessible manner to achieve real and sustained utility. Improvements in communications

BOX 2-9 RISK CHARACTERIZATION AND COMMUNICATION: DEVELOPING BETTER METHODS TO APPLY TO MANY ENVIRONMENTAL PROBLEMS

While it is well understood that risk assessments incorporate many sources of uncertainty, more needs to be done to ensure the accuracy and relevance of risk characterizations, including placing appropriate confidence limits on the estimates. It is also important to develop effective methods to convey variations and uncertainties in a way that the public can understand. The relationships between formal risk assessments and public perceptions of risks, the reliability of low-probability risk estimates, and modeling of human and organizational behavior in risk assessments are all poorly understood.

Faulty perception of risks can be costly. If minimal risks are assessed as being of serious concern, large financial expenditures may be wasted; if serious risks are assessed as minimal, significant public health or environmental damage may result. Differences between the "experts" and the public's perception of risks have led to controversy and conflict. Improving skill in risk assessment, management, and communication is important to human health, environmental protection, and the U.S. economy, since EPA spends hundreds of millions of dollars a year on research, and its regulations affect billions of dollars in expenditures and profits.

A number of significant factors must be better understood in order to develop better methods for characterizing and presenting risk estimates. These include the following:

- Processes by which scientists estimate the variability in their risk estimates: There is some evidence that scientists systematically underestimate the variability in their risk estimates (the 95% confidence limits are often too narrow) and perhaps systematically underestimate risks (Freudenburg, 1988). Also, certain kinds of consequences of adverse events often are unaccounted for in risk assessments. Freudenburg outlined questions concerning errors in risk estimates and suggested the research—much of it in social science—needed to understand the errors and reduce them.
- Processes by which the public arrives at its perceptions of risk: There is a large and growing literature dealing with how the public perceives risks and how it responds to others' attempts to communicate risks (e.g., NRC, 1994b, 1996c; Slovic, 1993).

technology, such as the Internet and World Wide Web data sites, will facilitate the dissemination of data, although these new channels also raise concerns about data quality and reliability.

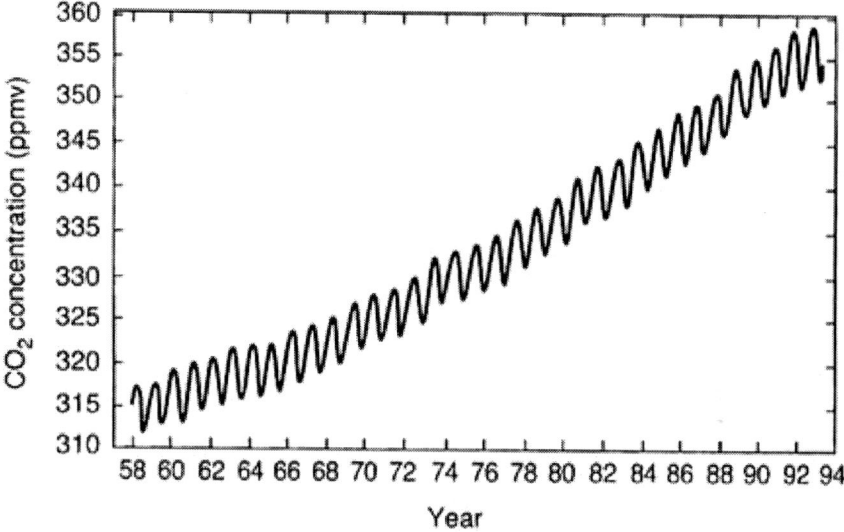

FIGURE 2-1 Accurate, sustained monitoring efforts at the Mauna Loa Observatory in Hawaii demonstrated rising levels of carbon dioxide in the atmosphere—an important piece of the climate change puzzle SOURCE: Schimel et al., 1995.

Figure 2-2 illustrates the activities that characterize a comprehensive environmental data acquisition and maintenance program. All of these activities are critical elements of the environmental research enterprise, requiring a high degree of scientific training and skill. They must be planned by people with the same capabilities and experience associated with the other core research components (process research and tool development). In particular, it is critical that both the scientists who will operate environmental monitoring networks and the scientists who plan to use the resulting data be involved in system design, system upgrade, data evaluation, and data dissemination (Box 2-10).

The call for better environmental monitoring has been heard in many quarters (e.g., EPA/SAB, 1988; NRC, 1995c). In addition, participants in a recent national forum whose aim was to identify environmental research priorities (summarized in *Linking Science and Technology to Society's Environmental Goals,* NRC, 1996a) identified environmental monitoring as one of six areas requiring increased attention in the future. The federal interagency Committee on Environmental and Natural Resources has also been taking action in this area. Despite the frequent calls for better environmental monitoring, current environmental monitoring programs are still inadequate for following environmental trends, evaluating management programs, and keeping records of global ecosystems.

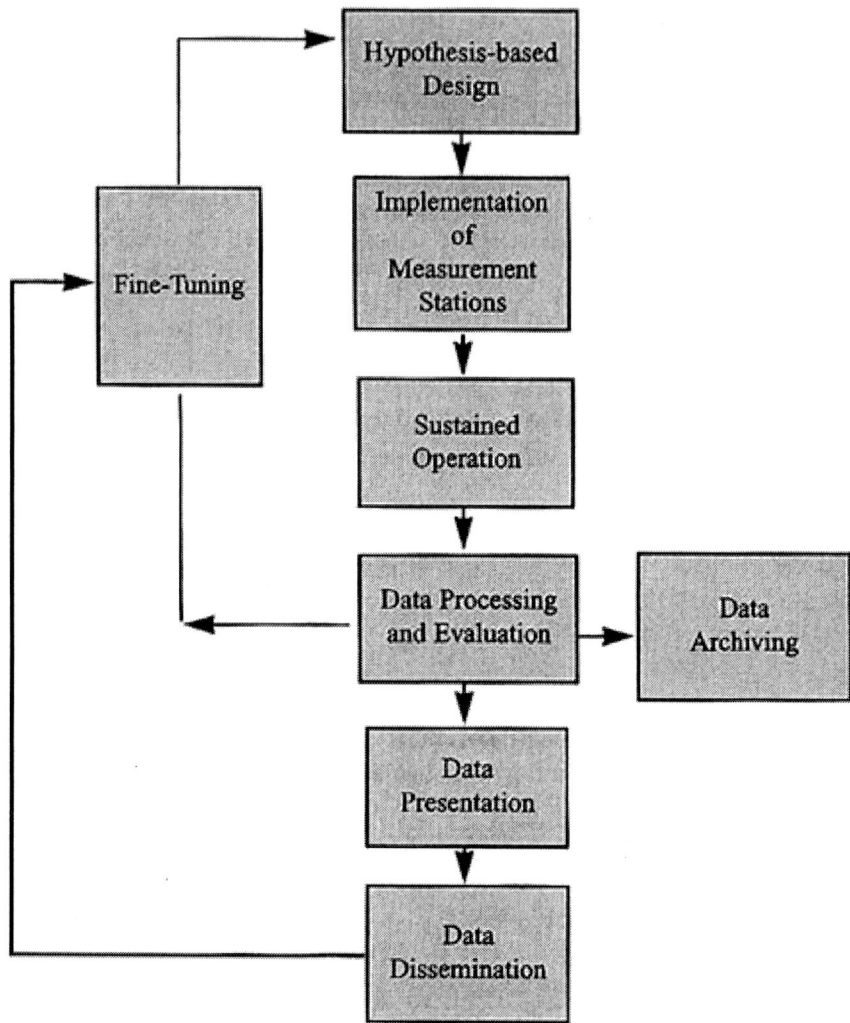

FIGURE 2-2 Elements of a successful environmental monitoring program.

IMPLEMENTING A CORE RESEARCH PROGRAM

The best way to deal successfully with the complexity of environmental issues and the rapid pace with which new issues can be expected to emerge is to direct a significant fraction of research funding into a core research program. It is essential that EPA and the nation gain a deeper understanding of underlying processes relevant to current and future environmental problems. Also essential is the development of innovative environmental research tools to assess and manage environmental problems and the acquisition of high-quality, long-term environmental data required for accurate and insightful assessment of environmental trends. These enhanced capabilities and the new depth of understanding that results will establish a credible scientific basis for environmental policies and enable EPA and the nation to respond more quickly, effectively, and efficiently to environmental problems. Although predicting or avoiding all environmental surprises will never be possible, the findings from core research will help society recognize and be prepared to effectively and efficiently address these problems as they emerge.

One of the advantages of core research is its focus on relatively fewer topics with broader applicability. This can be seen by comparing Tables 2-1 and 2-2. Table 2-1 is a list of specific, observed problems while Table 2-2 is a list of the kinds of environmental processes that define and underlie *all* environmental systems. Nevertheless, in a climate of limited resources, choices will have to be made even among core topics. This chapter identified a range of current and emerging issues and described some broad core research program areas worth pursuing. Difficult choices will have to be made, and it is essential that EPA develop the in-house capability necessary to make these choices.

Emphasis should be placed on projects with direct relevance to EPA's mission: investigations of risk assessment methodology are likely to take precedence over studies of human population control, although the latter is far from irrelevant to EPA. Cross-cutting, interdisciplinary studies that draw on findings from different fields will be of particular value. After broad program areas are selected, a key criterion for selecting research projects is the quality of the proposed science and the demonstrated ability of the investigators, as determined by a peer-review process.

Of course, many organizations other than EPA also play a role in carrying out elements of a core environmental research agenda. Priority should be placed on work not already well covered by other agencies and organizations, as discussed in Chapter 4.

Once key processes, tools, and data needs are identified, a multi-year commitment is needed to make progress on those topics. Priorities within core research are unlikely to change much over time. To realize the benefits of core research, it is necessary to "stay the course," allowing the difficult and often unpredictable nature of scientific investigation to play out. To be useful, data collection must be an ongoing effort.

Questions have arisen about EPA's ability to conduct a successful core environmental research program. However, the committee feels that it is crucial for the agency to maintain and enhance this capability. Since EPA will, by statute, be compelled to continue to pursue problem-driven environmental research in a

BOX 2-10 THE CHALLENGES OF LONG-TERM ECOSYSTEM MONITORING

A significant difficulty in studying the environment today is the lack of systematically collected historical information. An organized network of ecosystem monitoring systems is needed for several purposes including the following:

- assessment of the effectiveness of past actions, such as expenditures on wastewater treatment facilities, regulations restricting point sources of pollutants both to the atmosphere and to streams and lakes, and Superfund cleanup efforts;
- detection of trends in environmental indicators, such as carbon dioxide increases in the atmosphere;
- detection of continued unacceptable levels of pollutants in air and water;
- detection of threats to human health, such as pathogens in municipal water supplies and radon in indoor air; and
- creation of a baseline, or standard of variability, for environmental indicators such as temperature and precipitation, vegetation extent and type, and distribution, abundance, and diversity of plants and animals over long periods.

The task of designing an adequate ecosystems monitoring program is daunting. A host of chemicals found in the environment affect ecosystems and human health. In addition, information is needed for large numbers of organisms. The difficulty of developing an environmental monitoring program is in determining what to monitor, where, and for how long.

While in the past the federal government has monitored human disease outbreaks and has collected data on the weather, stream flow, and tides as basic information needed for societal planning, no similar data collection effort has ever been implemented and funded to monitor the condition of the broader environment. Several federal agencies have established limited ecosystem monitoring programs in the past decade. The USGS's National Water Quality Assessment Program serves to assess the quality of the country's ground and surface waters, and EPA's Environmental Monitoring and Assessment Program monitors eight resource types. In addition, NOAA monitors trends in long-lived atmospheric trace gases, the Forest Service's Forest Health Monitoring Program and NASA conduct satellite-and ground-based monitoring for ozone and other stratospheric gases. However, none of these programs is adequately integrated to provide the data needed for thorough environmental assessments.

Designing an effective environmental monitoring network requires substantial input from the scientists who will use the data. Environmental monitoring design should be hypothesis driven and linked to cutting edge

> research. The scientific community must also play key roles in implementation of the network and analysis of the results (NRC, 1995c).
>
> An effective monitoring network will require significant multidisciplinary and interagency cooperation. The sheer magnitude of the task and scarcity of resources call for agency programs to complement one another. Current cooperative efforts among federal agencies and the scientific community to integrate and coordinate monitoring activities, including work on compatibility of data from various activities, should be fostered.

variety of areas, EPA will need to draw on the insights and capabilities that an effective core environmental research program will yield. In practice, success in both problem-driven and core environmental research is dependent on the cross-fertilization achieved when scientists in the same organization or even the same scientists are vigorously pursuing both types of research activity.

At the same time that a solid program of core research is being established, decisions must be made about specific problems to be tackled in the problem-driven portion of the research program. As discussed above, problem-driven and core research are not separated by clear intellectual distinctions but rather by impetus and motivation. The former seeks to understand a single issue in depth and propose remedies, while the latter pursues the broad process knowledge, tool development, and data acquisition required to obtain a systematic and general understanding of the environment, including our effects on it and its effects on us. Findings in one area spark advances in the other in a continuous, mutually beneficial cycle, with both together achieving far more than each alone.

3

Achieving a Focused Research Agenda

Chapter 2 identified two types of environmental research, referred to as core research and problem-driven research, that are necessary to develop sound solutions to environmental problems and presented the case for the development and maintenance of core research capabilities. As discussed in Chapter 2, these categories are not mutually exclusive, but they do constitute a useful framework for describing the components of a comprehensive environmental research program. While a strong program to develop core capabilities is essential for anticipating some problems and better preparing the nation to solve *whatever* problems arise, problem-driven research (the focus of this chapter) that directly assists the agency in carrying out its regulatory mission will continue to be a necessary component of EPA's research program. Pressing problems with real and immediate economic, ecological, and health consequences must be addressed (see, for example, Box 3-1).

Recognizing that funding is not sufficient to examine every identified problem while also maintaining core research, it is important to avoid spreading research efforts so thin that no useful results can be obtained. Thus, EPA must prioritize within the long list of issues perceived as important, pursuing only the most critical in order to receive the biggest return on its research investment. Chapter 2 discussed a general approach for selecting the most important core research topics. This chapter discusses ways to identify and then select among problem-driven research areas.

ANTICIPATING EMERGING ENVIRONMENTAL PROBLEMS

Many advisory groups have proposed that efforts be made to identify emerging environmental issues and thus get a head start on avoiding or mitigating them (e.g., EPA/SAB, 1988, 1995). However, based on consideration of other reports

BOX 3-1 NUTRIENT CONTAMINATION OF COASTAL WATERS: ATTACKING A DIFFICULT PROBLEM

Maintaining the chemical and biological integrity of coastal waters in the face of an influx of nutrients and other pollutants generated by continuing demographic, economic, and technological growth in the watersheds of coastal areas has become a major challenge. Past efforts to protect coastal waters by addressing thermal pollution, soil loss and sediment control, toxic substances, and dredging have deflected attention from what is probably the most significant threat to many coastal waters—excessive nutrient loading. Nutrient inputs to aquatic ecosystems lead to deficiencies of dissolved oxygen. Degraded water quality, in turn, has significant negative impacts on biological resources, such as fish and shellfish. Rapid population growth, coastline development, increases in agricultural fertilization and the density of farm animals, and atmospheric inputs continue to increase the severity of the problem.

To mitigate nutrient contamination of coastal waters, problem-driven research is needed to answer questions such as the following:

- What are the details of the major routes of nitrogen from agriculture through the ground water into coastal regions? How might controls be effectively applied?
- What is known about the relationship between alternative land-management strategies and water quality? What is known about the relationships between regulations and incentives, such as zoning restrictions, tax incentives, and trading of pollution and other permits with a quota, and resulting land-use patterns and water quality?
- How can nitrogen inputs to drainage areas including those from atmospheric sources such as the combustion of fossil fuels be controlled, and what are the costs and benefits of potential control strategies?
- How is water quality related to nonpoint-source pollutant inputs such as those from agricultural and atmospheric sources? How are the biological resources of coastal areas related to water quality?
- How quickly, if at all, will coastal water quality improve following reduction of pollutant inputs?

Consistent monitoring and accurate modeling are also needed to understand natural cycles, ascertain anthropogenic sources of variability, indicate the efficacy of pollution control programs, delineate research needs, and identify potential problems as they begin to develop. Monitoring and modeling must be coordinated and interactive. A key task will be to characterize and quantify the nonpoint sources of contaminants.

Historical Problems	Chronic, Long-standing Problems	Current Problems	Emerging Problems	Potential Problems
(e.g., accumulation of horse manure on city streets, lead-based paint)	(e.g., urban air pollution, ground water contamination, soil erosion)	(e.g., *Cryptosporidium* in drinking water, loss of biodiversity, fine airborne particulates)	(e.g. environmental hormone modulators, climate-induced disease, multiple chemical exposure)	(e.g., harmful new products or chemicals, climate change)

FIGURE 3-1 Identification and mitigation of environmental problems is a continual process. The items listed as examples are simply illustrations of the type of environmental problems in each category. They are neither the only, nor necessarily the most important, problems.

and extensive discussion of the issues identified in Table 2-1, this committee concluded that there is a continuum of identified and emerging issues. The very fact that an issue has been recognized indicates that, in some circles at least, it has "emerged." The discovery and amelioration of environmental problems has been an ongoing process for hundreds of years. As illustrated in Figure 3-1, there is a continuum between well-defined, widely known problems and those that are less well understood and less well-known to a broad public. And beyond those, there are the speculative, potential future problems. Many observers have predicted that environmental problems of the future are likely to occur as a consequence of large-scale economic, demographic, and technological change. World population continues to increase, and the magnitude and patterns of human activities continue to evolve. In some regions, environmental problems are driven by rapid economic growth, increases in consumption, and technological change. This has been the pattern in the United States over the last 50 years. An ever-increasing percentage of the world's population lives in large urban areas. By the year 2000, there are likely to be more than 20 cities with populations exceeding 10 million, and most of these will be in developing countries (United Nations, 1992). Among the predictable consequences of this rapid growth are (1) the acceleration of geochemical cycles leading to effects such as climate change and the excessive fertilization of lacustrine, riverine, estuarine, and coastal ecosystems, (2) inefficient utilization of land resources leading to increased erosion, the destruction of productive land, and the physical impairment of ecosystems, (3) the introduction and accumulation of xenobiotic substances, and (4) re-emergence of infectious diseases once thought to be under control. Figure 3-2 illustrates some of the impacts of human population growth on global environmental change.

People transform the landscape and exploit natural resources, and yet our understanding of the nature of global ecosystems is just beginning to come into focus. Human society is dependent on the "goods and services" provided by

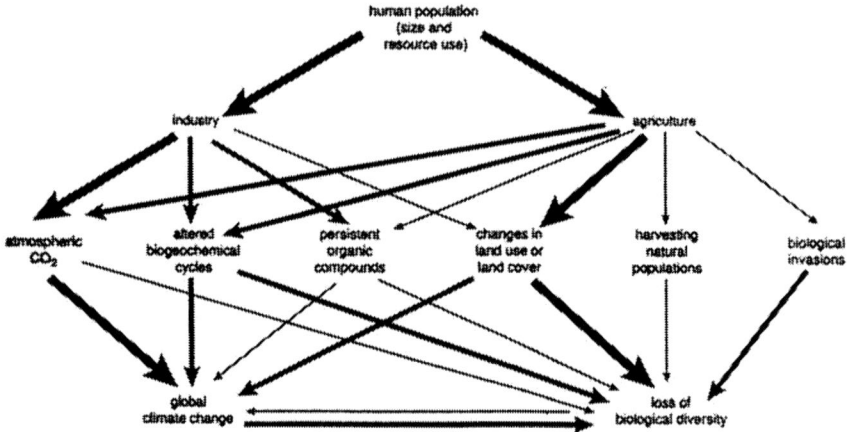

FIGURE 3-2 The growth of industry and agriculture in the past 200 years has promoted at least six identifiable components (*middle row*) of global environmental change. To varying degrees these components alter the earth's climate and reduce the planet's biological diversity. A general notion of the magnitude of these effects (*arrow thickness*) can be estimated, but the interrelationships and the synergistic effects of all six components have yet to be fully appreciated. SOURCE: Vitousek et al., 1996, as adapted from Vitousek, 1994.

ecosystems, including clean air, clean water, productive soils, and generation of food and fiber. A growing recognition of this dependence alters the way we conceptualize environmental problems. Reducing the harmful environmental impact of human activities on ecosystems, which in turn provide humans with essential goods and services, is of direct benefit to society.

In *Beyond the Horizon* (EPA/SAB, 1995), EPA's Science Advisory Board (SAB) suggested that EPA devote a substantial fraction of its resources to anticipating environmental problems that could emerge over the next 5 to 30 years and crafting preventive strategies. The SAB recommended that EPA incorporate "futures research and analysis" into its programs and activities and establish an "early warning system" to identify potential future environmental risks. The SAB suggested that EPA stimulate "coordinated national efforts to anticipate and respond to environmental change" and identified five areas worthy of focused attention: (1) sustainability of terrestrial ecosystems, (2) non-cancer human health effects, (3) total air pollutant loadings, (4) non-traditional environmental stressors, and (5) the health of the oceans.

Such "futures" analyses and evaluations must necessarily be based on educated assumptions about the nature of the relationship between the present and the future. The number and complexity of interactions in the global system cannot, at present, be modeled with precision, much less yield reliable predictions. It is increasingly recognized that the interactions between the planet, its non-human inhabitants, and its mobile, large, and still expanding human population constitute a dynamic system of rapidly increasing complexity. However, the sciences of chaos and complexity that may eventually prove helpful in understanding these interactions are still in their infancy and are as yet of limited predictive value. Two facts have emerged: (1) complex systems (such as the biogeosphere) exist at the interface between order and chaos and (2) linear cause-and-effect thinking yields highly unreliable extrapolations into the future. These observations reinforce the value of maintaining a broad core research program whose results will be applicable to a wide range of possible future environmental problems.

IDENTIFYING ENVIRONMENTAL PROBLEMS IN NEED OF FOCUSED ATTENTION

Even without anticipating the future problems, many existing environmental problems such as those listed in Table 2-1 and those described in Boxes 3-2 and 3-3, could benefit from scientific attention. These problems gain recognition in many ways: observation of direct effects on the public or environment, public demand, Congressional mandates, international negotiations, or identification as an actual or potential problem by organizations ranging from Worldwatch to EPA's SAB. EPA's program and regional offices also play an important role by identifying areas where technical assistance is needed for them to make sound regulatory, policy, or enforcement decisions. Finally, discoveries made in connection with core research programs often lead to the identification of previously unrecognized problems.

At present, EPA does not conduct any ongoing, systematic inventory of current and emerging problems. However, a thorough identification of issues is a necessary first step in selecting the right issues for attention. For this reason, some sort of continuous mechanism for soliciting current and emerging environmental issues from a wide range of sources, including an analysis of the implications of the latest research findings, is critical to EPA's research endeavor. It is not within this committee's charge to make recommendations concerning EPA's internal organization, but it is important for the agency to ensure that this function gets carried out.

The list of environmental issues identified by various individuals and organizations as important is very long, and continues to grow. Attention to all of these seemingly pressing issues of the day can quickly overwhelm a limited environmental research budget. Commitment, discipline, and a clear understanding of the value of maintaining *both* core and problem-driven research will be required for EPA to achieve an appropriately balanced, focused research program.

BOX 3-2 EFFECTIVENESS OF CONTROL STRATEGIES FOR TROPOSPHERIC OZONE

For more than 25 years, the products of photochemical smog—ozone (O_3), nitrogen dioxide (NO_2), peroxyacetyl nitrate (PAN) and peroxides, acid-bearing substances, and other trace gas species—have been the subject of environmental concern because of their effects on human health, vegetation, and, potentially, climate change. Ozone control programs initiated in the early 1970s in the United States to meet the National Ambient Air Quality Standard (NAAQS) (Clean Air Act, 42 USC Section 7401 7671q) have fallen far short of expectations, leaving more than 70 U.S. cities that fail to meet ozone standards and raising serious questions as to what might be the most cost-effective control program to pursue.

Many factors have contributed to the lack of progress in meeting the NAAQS for ozone. Greater urbanization and increased economic activity are obvious factors. Photochemical air quality simulation models are currently used as the principal approach for assessing emission control strategies to meet the ozone standard. However, the scientific soundness of these models and the quality of the required input data have been questioned. Additionally, although many sources of uncertainty in models and data have been identified, significant sources of error still remain.

To implement more effective pollution control strategies, further research and tools are required (NRC, 1991). Additional knowledge of atmospheric chemistry and the underlying quantitative relationship between ozone formation and anthropogenic emissions would be helpful. Also useful would be advances in understanding of the role of meteorology in the distribution and deposition of these atmospheric substances. Specific questions that need to be answered include the following: (1) How does ozone accumulation on local and regional scales depend on scale and location of the source and on meteorology? (2) What are the precursor relationships and contributions of anthropogenic emissions to local versus transported ozone production? (3) What are the precursor relationships and contributions of biogenic emissions to local versus transported ozone production? (5) What are the relationships between the control strategies designed to manage tropospheric ozone and those designed to manage other pollutant regimes of interest? (6) What is the role of new energy/transportation technologies in reducing ozone precursor emissions? (7) Can government stimulate the adoption of less polluting technologies?

Research tools that must be improved to make further progress in the mitigation of ozone air quality include instrumentation technology for the

> measurement of atmospheric concentrations and fluxes of ozone and its precursors; mathematical modeling and diagnostic analysis techniques for integration of the chemical and physical processes affecting the formation, distribution, and disposition of ozone in the environment; and laboratory studies for the determination of reaction rate coefficients and mechanistic pathways for ozone and its precursor species (NRC, 1991). Also important will be the deployment and operation of long-term monitoring networks designed specifically to (1) perform source attribution analyses on emissions of anthropogenic and biogenic volatile organic compounds and oxides of nitrogen, (2) track ozone and ozone precursor trends, and (3) characterize ozone exposures and NAAQS attainment. The development of data management, analysis, and distribution systems in support of the ozone attainment demonstration process will also be necessary.

CRITERIA FOR PRIORITIZING AMONG IDENTIFIED ISSUES

The notion of setting priorities when resources are limited is not a new one. It has been addressed by many others over time (e.g., EPA/SAB, 1988, 1990; NRC, 1994b, 1995a). This committee concludes that the concept of risk-based prioritization continues to be the strongest, most defensible approach for making such choices in the environmental arena. Two recent documents in particular (EPA/SAB, 1995; EPA, 1996) lay out useful criteria and processes for selecting among many environmental issues that appear to demand attention.

Beyond the Horizon, the 1995 report from the SAB, identified six issue-selection criteria (see Box 3-4). Five of these—timing, novelty, scope, severity, and probability—are particularly relevant to setting a focused environmental research agenda. The sixth, "visibility to the public," is less clearcut. Although it can influence perceptions of EPA's responsiveness to public concerns (Slovic, 1993), this factor has not historically corresponded well with the actual level of risk posed by a particular problem. The *Beyond the Horizon* criteria constitute a good, if rough, triage mechanism for narrowing the list to high-priority issues. However, a more detailed and quantitative approach also is needed. This is risk assessment. The 1996 strategic plan for EPA's Office of Research and Development (EPA, 1996) does a good job of laying out the principles of risk assessment as a mechanism for choosing among potential research issues. The risk assessment process is summarized in Figure 3-3.

Risk assessment methodologies are also in need of refinement. Large uncertainties can be introduced into risk assessment calculations due to inadequate data

BOX 3-3 DRINKING WATER DISINFECTION

Providing the public with safe potable water has been a responsibility of engineers, scientists, city managers, and public servants for centuries. This task has become increasingly difficult and complex as a result of demographic patterns, economic and technological growth, increased scientific understanding, and rising public expectations. One problem associated with this increasingly complicated task centers on disinfection byproducts (DBPs). All surface water supplies and many ground water supplies contain organic matter. They can also contain pathogenic organisms (viruses, bacteria, and protozoa). The importance of controlling these pathogens was brought home by recent outbreaks of infection in Milwaukee and Las Vegas, caused by *Cryptosporidium*, a particularly virulent protozoan (Singer, 1993).

Disinfection is required to provide biologically safe potable water; however, free chlorine, the classic disinfectant of choice in the United States, reacts with organic matter in the water to produce trihalomethanes and other chlorinated and brominated organic substances, known as DBPs. Several of these DBPs have been classified as probable human carcinogens. Other disinfectants, such as ozone and chlorine dioxide, can also produce potentially harmful DBPs. In general, the more vigorous the disinfection of a water supply with free chlorine or other chemical disinfectants, the fewer the pathogens but the greater the production of DBPs.

The challenge in potable water treatment and supply is to balance chemical risks with microbial risks, while also considering treatment and other costs. At present, this means regulating DBPs in drinking water while at the same time protecting the public from pathogens such as *Cryptosporidium*. Targeted problem-driven research is needed to clarify the chemical processes of the disinfectants, disinfectant combinations, and DBPs and to better understand their interactions with water and organic material. Core research in the areas of risk analysis methodology and comparative risk assessment, core tools such as analytical methods and capabilities, and better monitoring approaches will also provide important information.

Together, problem-driven and core research would greatly improve our ability to address the following significant questions: (1) How can we more accurately detect and quantitatively measure DBPs in treated water supplies? (2) How can detection and quantitative measurement of pathogens in raw and treated water supplies be improved? (3) How can we develop improved risk analysis methodologies for carcinogens? (4) How can we develop comparative risk assessments for different issues, such as comparison of chemical risks from carcinogens with biological risks from human pathogens? (5) How can we develop improved and cost-effective treatment technologies for both large and small water supply systems?

> **BOX 3-4 CRITERIA FOR SELECTING AMONG IDENTIFIED ENVIRONMENTAL ISSUES[1]**
>
> *Timing*: How soon is this problem likely to emerge, how important is early recognition, and how rapidly can the problem be reversed?
>
> *Novelty*: To what extent is this a new problem that has not been addressed adequately?
>
> *Scope*: How extensive—in terms of geography or population affected, for example—is this problem?
>
> *Severity*: How intensive are the likely health, ecological, economic, and other impacts of this problem, and are they reversible?
>
> *Visibility*: How much public concern is this problem likely to arouse?
>
> *Probability*: What is the likelihood of this problem emerging, and necessitating a response, in the future?
>
> ---
>
> [1] From *Beyond the Horizon: Using Foresight to Protect the Environmental Future* (EPA/SAB, 1995). Committee opinion is divided as to whether "visibility," i.e., public perception, is an appropriate criterion for selecting among research topics.

inputs. In addition there are uncertainties in risk assessments due to a fundamental lack of understanding of the biology involved. Each underlying assumption in risk assessment contains some inherent uncertainty, but the cumulative level of uncertainty is often not quantified or adequately communicated in risk estimates. Developing reproducible, quantitative measures to characterize the uncertainty has not been possible. A research agenda based on risk assessment must compare the magnitudes of various risks, but there are currently no well-developed consensus methods for such comparative risk assessment. Application of a credible method for comparative risk would allow EPA to focus its research efforts on those problems whose solution is likely to bring the greatest benefit to human and/or environmental health. Achieving a better understanding of risk and developing better methods for performing risk assessments were identified as core research needs in Chapter 2.

Just a few of the unanswered questions surrounding the performance and communication of comparative risk assessments are:

(1) Can (and should) voluntary risks be compared with involuntary risks and, if so, under what circumstances?

(2) How can comparative risk assessments be communicated effectively without creating the perception that some risks are being downplayed?

(3) Is it necessary and sufficient to have a common currency of risk, such as probability of death or expected dollar cost?7

(4) How should risks of differing or large uncertainties be compared?

Despite these shortcomings, risk assessment currently is the most satisfactory approach for setting research priorities in the environmental arena. It is particularly valuable in identifying areas of uncertainty that need to be resolved in order to achieve more accurate assessments.

In the absence of reliable risk assessment, enormous sums of money that might be better spent elsewhere may be allocated to dealing with *perceived* risks. While it is essential to ensure public health and environmental integrity, limited resources reinforce the need to assess risks as accurately as possible (see Box 3-5). Estimates have indicated that the cost of environmental regulations in the

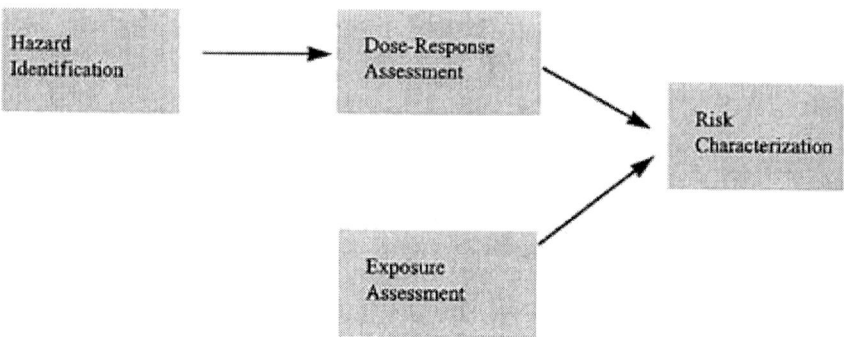

FIGURE 3.3 The risk assessment process. The process consists of four steps:
1. During *hazard identification,* scientists describe the adverse effects (e.g., short-term illness, cancer, reproductive effects) that might occur due to exposure to the environmental stressor of concern.
2. During *dose-response assessment,* scientists estimate the toxicity or potency of a stressor. The dose-response assessment attempts to quantify the relationship between the amount of exposure to a stressor and the extent of injury or disease.
3. During *exposure assessment,* scientists describe the nature and size of the populations(s) or ecosystem(s) potentially exposed to a stressor and the probable magnitude and duration of exposure. Exposure assessment includes a description of the pathways by which the stressor might travel through the environment; the changes that a stressor undergoes en route; the environmental concentrations of the stressor relative to time, distance, and direction from its source; potential routes of exposure (oral, dermal, or inhalation); and the distribution of sensitive subgroups, such as pregnant women and children.
4. During *risk characterization,* scientists use the data collected in the three previous steps to estimate the effects of human or ecological exposure to the stressor of concern. They estimate the likelihood that a population will experience any of the adverse effects associated with the stressor under known or expected conditions of exposure. This estimate can be qualitative (e.g., high or low probability) or quantitative (e.g., one in a million probability of occurrence) and is highly dependent on the accuracy of the first three steps.
SOURCE: EPA, 1996, as adapted from *Risk Assessment in the Federal Government: Managing the Process* (NRC, 1983), and *Science and Judgment in Risk Assessment* (NRC, 1994b).

> **BOX 3-5 ENVIRONMENTAL ENDOCRINE MODULATORS: REDUCING UNCERTAINTIES**
>
> A variety of naturally occurring and synthetic chemicals have been identified as having hormonal effects on many species of animals. Many of these chemicals, referred to as endocrine modulators, are released into the environment by human activity. Because humans depend on ecological systems for goods and services, and because federal laws prohibit damage to ecological systems, it is essential to determine to what degree such chemicals threaten ecological systems. The potential for harm to ecosystems, wildlife, and humans must be judged correctly to avoid wasteful and unnecessary expenditures of time, money, and human resources.
>
> To assess the risk of endocrine modulators in the environment, problem-driven research is needed to resolve significant uncertainties concerning the distribution of such chemicals in the environment; sources of chemicals and their fate and transport in natural systems; concentrations at which different chemicals affect wildlife species; and the extent, nature, and time scale of ecological effects or potential effects.
>
> Understanding the chemical, physical, natural or anthropogenic changes that affect ecological systems would be easier if a long-term monitoring network were in place. Extensively studied, relatively pristine sites are also helpful, as they can be used to provide a frame of reference for comparing systems affected by toxicants. EPA's plan to identify 30 to 40 sites for long-term study and monitoring will ultimately help clarify concerns about endocrine modulators as well as other potentially toxic substances.

United States will total between $171 and $185 billion by the year 2000 (Carlin et al., 1992). Compliance with air pollution control regulations will cost an estimated $94 billion per year by the year 2000 (Carlin et al., 1992). Russell et al. (1991) estimated that cleaning up all the major hazardous-waste sites would cost between $500 billion and $1 trillion over the next 30 years. The sums are enormous, and a convincing analysis must be provided to demonstrate that these expenditures are justified as the most cost-effective way to reduce risks to human health and to the environment.

DEVELOPING AND MAINTAINING RISK ASSESSMENT CAPABILITIES AT EPA

As described both in the ORD strategic plan (EPA, 1996) and in the discussion above, consistent, thorough, well-grounded risk assessments are fundamental to EPA's research strategy. Thus, it is important to have strong, internal capabilities in this area. It will not be helpful to the agency in the long run to rely exclusively on outsiders for issue selection and prioritization. As was made clear in assembling Table 2-1, each attempt by an outside group to identify high priority research issues yields different results due to the nature of each group's composition, the evolution of issues, and variations in methods used. Although independent oversight and advice is valuable for any organization, no external advisory group can substitute for the value of having an experienced, in-house, issue selection team to complement the issue-identification function described above.

RETAINING FLEXIBILITY

The discussion of core research in Chapter 2 emphasized the importance of "staying the course"—the fundamental processes in need of elucidation, the research tools required, and the kinds of data needed do not change much from year to year. For problem-driven research the opposite is true. *It is essential to re-evaluate and re-prioritize among such research projects at regular intervals to ensure that limited resources are being directed at the most important, high-risk issues.* In fact, one of the functions of problem-driven research is to reduce the uncertainties associated with particular identified problems—uncertainties that may have led to inaccurate initial risk assessments and thus inappropriate responses. Periodically, some environmental issues can be moved off the priority list to make room for problems that pose higher risks or for *potentially* risky problems with large uncertainties that remain to be resolved. The problem-driven portion of a research program must be designed with enough flexibility and with appropriate adaptive feedback capabilities to cope with periodic changes in direction when necessary.

4

EPA's Position in the Broader Environmental Research Enterprise

EPA'S ROLE IN RESEARCH

EPA is an important entity in the environmental regulatory arena, and its research efforts are influential in the advancement of environmental knowledge. But the agency is not by any means alone among government and private organizations conducting environmental research. EPA conducts approximately $500 million out of approximately $5 billion of federally supported environmental research annually. Other organizations involved in environmental research are shown in Figure 4-1. It is in EPA's interest to be an active participant in inter-agency and interorganizational research to assure that the agency (1) receives from and transmits to other organizations relevant research information of mutual interest and (2) maintains a credible research program that is supportive of EPA's mandated regulatory activities while staying within the agency's budget. Given limited resources and the magnitude of the challenge, EPA must adopt a highly selective approach in guiding research pursuits. This chapter focuses on EPA's evolving research mission as it relates to the work of other organizations that also conduct environmental research.

PARTNERSHIPS WITH OTHER GOVERNMENT ORGANIZATIONS AND THE PRIVATE SECTOR

Understanding and successfully addressing complex environmental problems requires extensive research over a broad range of scientific disciplines (see, for example, Box 4-1). EPA cannot (and should not) by itself develop and apply all the knowledge needed to discharge its mandate, because its resources are not sufficient and because other agencies, private companies, and universities, in the United States and abroad, are also engaged in information gathering and analysis.

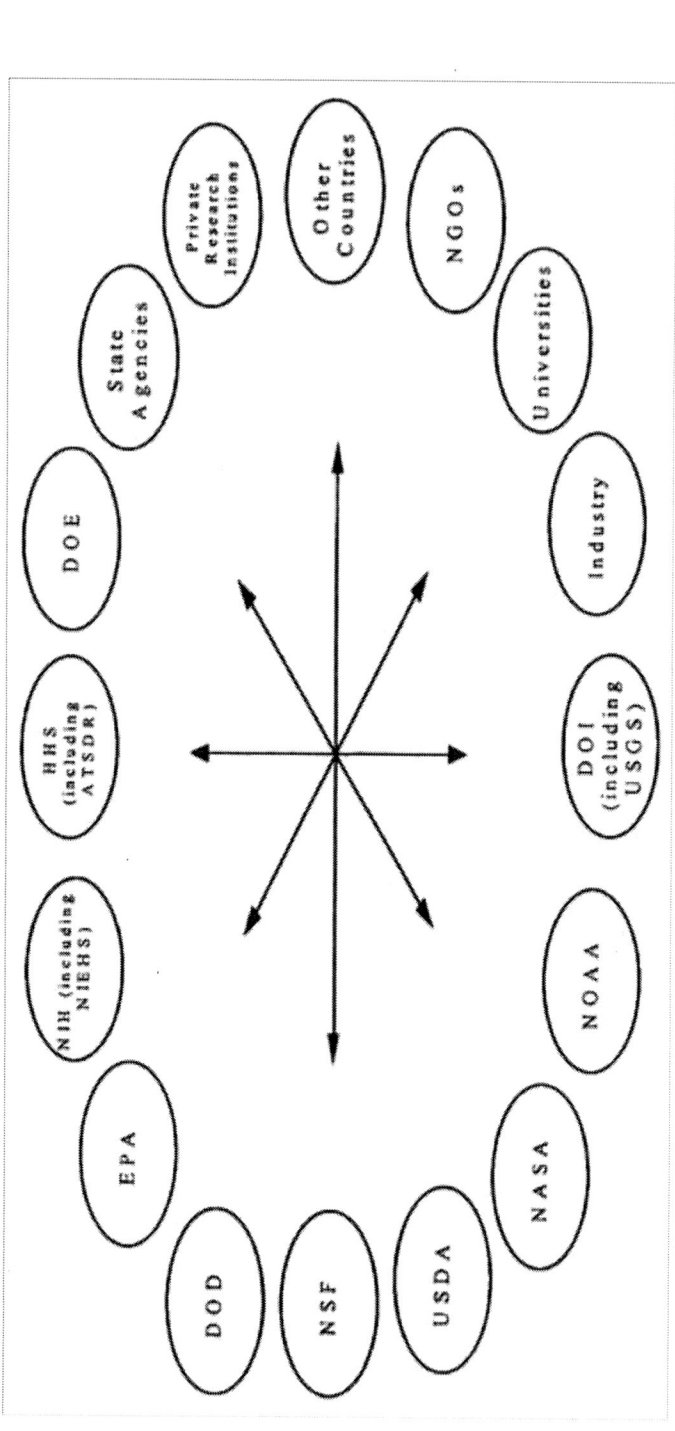

FIGURE 4-1 Some of the many partners in the environmental research endeavor. Acronyms: NOAA, National Oceanic and Atmospheric Administration; NASA, National Aeronautics and Space Administration; USDA, U.S. Department of Agriculture; NSF, National Science Foundation; DOD, Department of Defense; NIH, National Institutes of Health; NIEHS, National Institute of Environmental Health Sciences; HHS, Department of Health and Human Services; ATSDR, Agency for Toxic Substances and Disease Registry; DOE, Department of Energy; NGOs, nongovernment organizations; DOI, Department of the Interior; USGS, U.S. Geological Survey

BOX 4-1 GLOBAL CLIMATE CHANGE: A LARGE-SCALE, COMPLEX PROBLEM REQUIRES AN INTERDISCIPLINARY, MULTI-AGENCY APPROACH

Atmospheric scientists have recently concluded that changes in atmospheric composition, driven by agricultural and industrial emissions of "greenhouse gases," (primarily carbon dioxide and methane) are almost certainly causing a measurable warming of the earth's surface and lower atmosphere (IPCC, 1996). Furthermore, these scientists have concluded that scattering of incident sunlight by atmospheric aerosols, due to industrial emissions and biomass burning, has counteracted some of the potential warming. Current programs (driven by acid deposition and human health concerns) aimed at reducing atmospheric aerosol levels could therefore result in global warming beyond that already observed (IPCC, 1996).

As the climate warms, it may affect ecosystem viability, managed crop and forest yields, and human health. Changes could be induced both by shifts in mean temperatures and by the increases in extreme weather conditions (drought, flood, severe storms) that climate models predict will occur for many regions. Current models have demonstrated the key role that the hydrologic system plays in climate change and the dramatic impact that significant climate change may have on regional freshwater availability and quality. Exploratory studies have also suggested strong feedbacks between climate change and the ecology of many ecosystems (IPCC, 1996).

While it is clear that global warming is occurring, the degree to which it will continue to occur, what actions are stimulating it, and what actions will ameliorate unfavorable change are all still uncertain. Scientists are also very unsure about the future ramifications of global warming. Possible scenarios include rising sea levels from melting polar ice caps leading to coastal flooding, changes in precipitation patterns leading to drought in some regions, and the loss of plant and/or animal species unable to migrate fast enough to follow shifting climate conditions into regions where the species would remain acclimated. Suggestions that climate change may also have a significant impact on the rate and mechanisms of disease spread also need to be investigated (IPCC, 1996).

The processes that need to be investigated to adequately characterize global warming are far beyond the capabilities of EPA or any single agency. Rather, addressing the range of environmental problems related to global climate change will require an integrated, multi-agency effort. So far, the rate of global warming and global warming's impact on meteorological and hydrological systems as well as on terrestrial vegetation

> have been the main focus of climate change research. In the future, more extensive research into environmental strategies and technology to lessen the emissions of greenhouse gases and to mitigate the undesirable hydrological, ecological, and health effects of climate change will be required. EPA can, and should, take a lead role in efforts to predict the ecological, health, and economic impacts of climate change and in the design of strategies to mitigate or remedy effects of climate change. One area, in particular, that EPA, together with other agencies, should consider is the establishment of a wide range of long term monitoring systems for key chemical, meteorological, hydrological, ecological, and health parameters. The data from these monitoring systems will need to be archived and analyzed to track the rate and impacts of climate change.

Additional cooperative research efforts between EPA and other organizations could lead to more effective solutions and policies to address environmental problems.

EPA must continue to be a significant partner in the national and international research effort, supporting and carrying out both core and problem-driven research as previously described. However, while EPA needs to retain in-house research capabilities, it should also learn from, use, and not needlessly duplicate research conducted or sponsored by other entities. Cooperating in research endeavors can provide all involved parties with a sense of working toward a common purpose as well as with access to more information. A collective effort can yield results far greater than the sum of individual, isolated endeavors.

EPA has demonstrated that it can effect successful research collaborations, and it is encouraged to continue and expand such activities. Illustrative examples include the following:

- The establishment of a joint EPA-NSF competitive grants programs in water and watersheds; technology for a sustainable environment; and valuation studies for environmental policy. These programs highlight the need for broad interdisciplinary environmental research and take advantage of the NSF's engagement of the very broad scientific community and experience with peer review.
- The restoration of the Merrimack River, assisted by a grant and technical help from EPA as well as the involvement of the New Hampshire River Protection Program and other local organizations.
- Work done jointly with the USGS in support of the agencies' efforts in

water quality monitoring and assessment to provide a nationally consistent description of current water quality conditions for the nation's water resources.
- The establishment of the American Institute of Chemical Engineering Center for Waste Reduction Technologies, an industry/government research partnership whose focus includes research and technology development and its application to industrial processes to significantly reduce their impact on the environment.
- The establishment of the Health Effects Institute, a public-private partnership between the EPA and 28 manufacturers or marketers of motor vehicles or engines, whose focus is to provide decision makers, scientists, and the public with high-quality scientific information that helps to impartially answer key questions about health effects from motor vehicle emissions and other sources of air pollution.
- The co-leadership role of EPA in the North American Research Strategy for Tropospheric Ozone, a composite organization whose membership spans government, the utilities industry, and academia in Mexico, the United States, and Canada. The program's primary mission is to coordinate and enhance scientific research and assessment of tropospheric ozone behavior, with the central programmatic goal of determining workable, efficient, and effective strategies for local and regional ozone control.
- The coordination of research activities and collaboration with other scientists from federal, state, and local agencies and other organizations demonstrated in EPA's Environmental Monitoring and Assessment Program (EMAP).

There are many areas in which industry, academic institutions, and consulting firms should and do develop important solutions to environmental problems, such as industrial pollution prevention approaches and life-cycle analyses to reduce the creation of pollutants and unusable residues. In areas where the private sector can perform the bulk of the research, EPA should continue to have a minimal level of involvement. Through partnerships (including personnel exchanges), EPA can stay abreast of emerging technologies, evaluate new approaches, and provide a broad knowledge base.

STRENGTHENING SCIENTIFIC CAPACITY AT EPA

Recognizing that private sector interests do not always coincide with the full range of national interests, EPA should concentrate its own research and grants programs in areas where the private sector has little incentive to conduct research or develop better solutions to environmental problems. Examples include municipal wastewater and drinking water treatment, nonpoint-source pollution control, restoration of degraded ecosystems, and large-scale regional and global air pollution problems. No one company, industry, or municipality has a unique stake in these issues, making risk reduction research and evaluation of control options hard to justify to management or investors. These are areas of "public good" for which a national agency like EPA should have lead responsibility and undertake the relevant research.

Cooperative research ventures require the open sharing of both information and ideas. Reflecting appreciation for this, EPA has established and should continue a series of interdisciplinary workshops on topics relevant to environmental protection, effectively serving as a link between various research groups both inside and outside of EPA. Whether EPA has research results to share or not, EPA personnel can participate in such discussions to assess whether and, if so, how new information can be applied to EPA's immediate concerns. Also, EPA can assess which topics need more research and in turn can establish new priorities. These workshops promote a dynamic process for shaping environmental research priorities and thus contribute to protecting human health and the quality of our environment.

For EPA to play its most productive role, however, it must stimulate the development of its own science capacity through proper incentives and realistic resource commitments to its research staff. (A second NRC committee, the Committee on Research and Peer Review at EPA, will consider these issues in much greater detail. See Chapter 1, "History and Purpose of this Study.") EPA researchers should be required to have knowledge of the basic processes and tools critical to environmental systems and have the ability to apply this knowledge to important environmental issues. In addition, the ability of EPA researchers to then articulate and transfer this knowledge to support the development and implementation of environmental policy is critical to the agency's mission.

The committee recommends that EPA ensure research staff participation in interagency coordination efforts and in scientific meetings and conferences and provide incentives and rewards to those who seek out and work with their counterparts in other organizations. This cooperation must be accompanied by information that more clearly describes EPA's research program. To facilitate cooperation with others, as well as to improve its internal planning, EPA should compile an easily understood annual summary of its research strategy and programs. The report should be organized into broad categories of core and problem-driven research, with subcategories describing specific program areas. The absence of such a report makes it difficult to fully understand or evaluate EPA's research program.

A financial commitment to core research, wherever it is conducted, is essential if it is to be sustained. A long-term financial commitment also will make possible the support of the required technical and administrative staff to effectively and efficiently manage the nation's environmental programs. The committee did not have the time or necessary data to fully determine the optimal magnitude of a desirable core program, nor was it asked to do so. However, based on many decades of experience and observation, the committee believes that there should be a roughly even balance between the core research program and problem-driven research projects.

IMPROVING COOPERATIVE DATA COLLECTION AND EVALUATION

Environmental data is collected for a variety of purposes by many entities, generally for the purposes of describing the status of, and changes to, environmental resources over time, to confirm compliance with regulations, or to serve as an indicator of potential future change. In addition, environmental monitoring is required for the retrospective evaluation of the effectiveness of various past environmental policies and actions. Acquiring, archiving, and making environmental data easily accessible should be a priority for EPA. Increasing collaborations among EPA and other organizations that collect environmental data is essential for optimizing the use of existing data and identifying what types of additional data collection efforts are needed.

Data collection is a large, difficult challenge, and EPA is commended for its efforts to coordinate its data collection activities with those of other agencies such as NIEHS, USGS, and other bureaus of the DOI, NOAA (including the National Weather Service), NASA, the National Cancer Institute, the Forest Service, the Natural Resources Conservation Service of the USDA, and the Centers for Disease Control. Indeed, EPA is encouraged to press ahead with efforts to develop a national environmental monitoring program working with the Office of Science and Technology Policy and other agencies.

Monitoring databases provide histories of environmental change and can be examined to ascertain the statistical relationships between human activities and environmental responses, between regulations and pollutant types and inputs, and between human responses and different types of incentives or disincentives designed to influence voluntary actions affecting the environment. Monitoring for retrospective evaluation seeks to find effects by detecting changes in the status and condition of some organism, population, or community. It does not assume any knowledge of cause-effect relationships, although the intention is usually to establish a cause if an effect is found. Through monitoring and retrospective evaluations, EPA, other federal agencies, the Congress, and the public can gain insight into improved ways to achieve environmental goals. This process promotes a shift from a static view of regulations to a dynamic, evolving view that regulations have a finite lifetime and are in need of periodic reassessment.

Monitoring and retrospective evaluation of environmental policies can be most effectively done via partnerships between EPA and other organizations, whose missions complement or overlap that of EPA's. EPA should initiate a retrospective monitoring and evaluation program making sure to take maximum advantage of existing data bases. A good example of a potentially useful retrospective analysis might be an assessment of the relationship between wastewater treatment and downstream water quality changes. Other retrospective studies could assess pesticide contaminant levels in ground water as related to agricultural

BOX 4-2 LONG-TERM STUDIES LEAD TO UNDERSTANDING OF COMPLEX INTERACTIONS[1]

The results of two long-term environmental studies (Schindler et al., 1996; Yan et al., 1996) published in *Nature* in 1996 have shown that the penetration of lake waters by harmful ultraviolet radiation is related to climate warming and acid rain, as well as to depletion of stratospheric ozone. The interactions between these environmental stresses are complex, and these studies are of exceptional interest because environmental problems are seldom subjected to this sort of analysis (Tilman, 1989).

Schindler et al. added sulfuric acid to lakes in the Experimental Lakes Area of northwestern Ontario that they had been studying and in some cases manipulating for two decades. They showed that both acid levels and climate warming over the past 20 years have led in different and complex ways to declines in dissolved organic carbon (DOC) compounds in lake waters. DOCs absorb solar radiation, including UV-B, and their decline has permitted radiation to penetrate much deeper into the water. The effect was particularly evident in clear, shallow lakes, which are common in the boreal zone (the huge northern temperate zone of coniferous forests) and even more so in arctic and alpine regions, and it outweighed the effect of ozone depletion in exposing aquatic organisms to damage by UV-B radiation. Schindler and colleagues noted further that in such lakes some of the biological damage attributed to acid deposition may instead have been caused by UV-B exposure.

In the second long-term study, Yan et al. monitored the ecological conditions of Swan Lake in northern Ontario. The lake has been subjected to severe atmospheric deposition of sulfur from smelter fumes from nearby copper and nickel mines, and substantial amounts of sulfur have been stored in sediments. During a two-year drought in 1986 and 1987, the water level dropped considerably so that the lake's surface area shrank by 18%. This led to oxidation of the sulfur compounds contained in the uppermost layer of exposed near-shore sediments to sulphuric acid. In the subsequent wet year, the acid washed into the lake and lowered its pH greatly, from 5.8 before the drought to 4.5 in the year after. DOC declined by a factor of three, in part directly by acidification and in part by settling out after aggregation with sedimentary aluminum released by the acidification. Because of the decline in DOC, the depth of the lake exposed to at least 1% of surface UV-B radiation increased from 1.8 m in 1987 to 5.6 m in 1988, corresponding to 94% of lake volume.

These studies illustrate that three anthropogenic stresses on the environment—climate warming, acid deposition, and ozone depletion—are

---

[1] Adapted from Gorham, 1996.

> linked to one another through their influence in deepening the penetration of UV-B radiation into clear-water lakes. It is likely that this influence will increase as ozone depletion worsens, climate continues to warm, and sulfur compounds, stored in lake sediments and wetland peats, oxidize in response to falling water tables. Clearly, the physical, chemical, and biological processes of diverse environmental impacts are complex and inextricably linked to one another, requiring an integrated, whole-ecosystem approach to their study. Long-term investigations, often lasting decades, are necessary to enhance understanding of such complicated environmental problems.

management practices or review a wetland restoration site to judge the degree to which restoration was successful.

A great challenge remains in the selection of appropriate indicators useful for monitoring ecosystems. A recently initiated NRC study on this topic, sponsored by EPA, should assist EPA and others in determining what aspects of environmental conditions and trends should be monitored for various purposes, what is known about successful biological indicators, what aspects of ecosystems have been particularly difficult to develop useful indicators for, and where research is most likely to yield useful results.

Another difficult challenge related to environmental monitoring where EPA could play a major role is in the development of more comprehensive models of integrated environmental systems. The development of integrated environmental models in conjunction with data collected from strategically designed monitoring networks will lead to more cost-effective multi-media approaches for managing and sustaining environmental quality. Long-term ecological studies are useful for developing such models and are essential for understanding the complex interactions within ecosystems (see Box 4-2).

In summary, it is essential that EPA maintain a research staff, but it is also essential that this staff focus on research areas not already being extensively investigated by others. Cooperation with other organizations through joint research programs, grant programs, sponsorship of workshops, joint collection and evaluation of data, and other efforts is essential so that EPA and the nation can achieve maximum value from the agency's research investments.

5

Summary, Conclusions, and Recommendations

SUMMARY

Pressures on the environment will continue to increase. Global population increase, rising incomes, and agricultural and industrial expansion will inevitably produce unanticipated and potentially deleterious ecological, economic, and human health consequences. Environmental research has proven its value in helping to respond to and prevent many environmental problems, and it continues to be a wise and necessary investment.

The charge to this committee was to provide an overview of significant emerging environmental issues; identify and prioritize research themes and projects that are most relevant to understanding and resolving these issues; and consider the role of EPA's research program in addressing these issues, in the context of research being conducted or sponsored by other organizations. After careful deliberation, the committee decided *not* to simply present a limited list of "emerging" issues with specific research projects to address them. Such an exercise would provide a mere snapshot in time, based on the insights of one particular collection of individuals. Instead—and hopefully more valuably—this report provides an overview of important environmental issues and presents a framework for organizing environmental research. The report also describes major research themes and programs of relevance to EPA; suggests criteria that can be used to identify and prioritize among important research areas; recommends actions EPA should take to build its scientific capacity; and provides illustrations of the kinds of research projects that EPA should consider.

CONCLUSIONS

As a key environmental agency, EPA needs to support and maintain a strong research program. An evolving understanding of the complexity, magnitude, and inter-relatedness of environmental problems leads us to conclude that a new balance of research programs may be helpful. This report describes a framework for conducting research in a way that will help alleviate the problems of the moment while providing a basis for solving tomorrow's problems.

In the past, pressing environmental issues have been addressed primarily through focused research efforts directed toward solving particular problems. Although this approach to environmental research can be effective, has often been necessary, and will surely continue, it also has limitations. In order to address the abundance of established, emerging, and as-yet-unknown environmental issues, an expanded understanding of the scientific principles underlying environmental systems is needed. Achieving this understanding will require innovative, interdisciplinary approaches.

To develop the knowledge needed to address current and emerging environmental issues, EPA should undertake both *problem-driven research* and *core research*. Problem-driven research is targeted at understanding and solving identified environmental problems, while core research aims to provide broader, more generic information that will help improve understanding of many problems now and in the future. Core research includes three components: (1) understanding the processes that drive and connect environmental systems; (2) development of innovative tools and methods for understanding and managing environmental problems; and (3) long-term collection and dissemination of accurate environmental data.

Research activities within problem-driven and core research programs may often overlap. Fundamental discoveries can be made during the search for a solution to a narrowly defined problem; likewise, as illustrated earlier in this report, breakthroughs in problem-solving often occur as a result of core research efforts. Both kinds of investigations are needed, and feedback between them will greatly enhance the overall environmental research endeavor (see Figure 5-1).

Because EPA's task of protecting the environment and human health is so vast and difficult, and because resources to undertake the necessary research are very limited, choices will have to be made among many worthwhile projects. The approaches for making these choices will be different in the core and problem-driven portions of the research program. The former should seek better understanding of fundamental phenomena and generate broadly relevant research tools and information. The latter will be more responsive to regulatory activities and other immediate needs and should be guided by the paradigm of risk reduction. Because there are so many specific issues of importance to the public, the Congress, and EPA's own program and regional offices, there is a temptation to include many problems for attention. It is important to resist this trend: it will inevitably lead either to the dilution of efforts to solve the most pressing problems or to the reduction of funding available for critical core research needs.

Interactions among the natural environment, plants, animals, and the evergrowing human population are highly complex and inherently unpredictable. Although this report provides a broad overview of current and emerging environmental issues, it is important to note that this is merely a snapshot in time. Identification of issues requiring attention is a dynamic, continuous process.

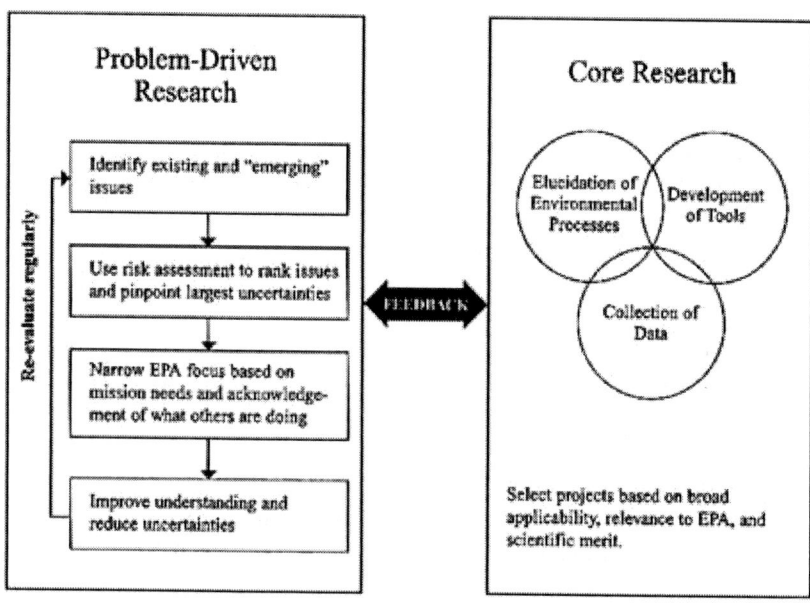

FIGURE 5-1 A framework for environmental research at EPA.

With its limited budget, staff, and mandate, it is not possible or reasonable for EPA to act alone in understanding and addressing all environmental problems. Many other federal agencies, state agencies, other organizations (including utilities), universities, and private companies have played and will continue to play important roles in environmental research. Cooperation with others will be particularly needed in the area of environmental monitoring, a complex and costly undertaking, and in the investigation of global-scale issues.

Another factor to consider in determining EPA's research role on a particular environmental issue is whether the private sector has any incentive to study or develop better solutions, or whether the primary research must originate from the public sector to serve the public good. Examples of areas of "public good" that might deserve EPA attention include municipal wastewater and drinking water treatment, nonpoint-source pollution control, restoration of degraded ecosystems, and large-scale regional and global air pollution problems.

RECOMMENDATIONS

To enhance the productivity and effectiveness of EPA's research efforts, the committee makes recommendations in three areas: a general approach to research, core research themes, and problem-driven research themes.

Approach to Research

- **EPA should establish a balance between problem-driven and core research.** Although there is currently an emphasis on problem-driven research projects in EPA, the core component of EPA's research program should be developed to be approximately equal in magnitude.
- **EPA should develop an internal mechanism for continually identifying emerging issues and then applying a risk assessment evaluation to these issues to determine the highest priorities and areas of greatest uncertainty.** One important method for identifying emerging issues is to review and synthesize new findings from the core research program. EPA research personnel should be fully engaged in the issue identification and research planning process.
- **EPA should cooperate closely with agencies, organizations, municipalities, universities, and industries involved in environmental research.** In addition to providing research support, mechanisms for cooperation might include participation of EPA management in interagency coordination efforts, participation of staff in scientific meetings and conferences, and incentives and rewards for individuals who seek out and work with their counterparts in other organizations. Collaboration should be maintained in research endeavors, environmental monitoring, data archiving, and environmental policy formulation and evaluation. EPA should continue to act as a coordinator in bringing various environmental researchers together to exchange information and ideas, possibly in the form of interdisciplinary workshops on particular environmental topics. This would also help in "scanning the horizon" to identify new environmental trends and emerging problems. Through these meetings, EPA can discuss the relative risks as well as solutions and policies and can determine which areas require more research.
- **EPA should compile, publish, and disseminate an annual summary of all research being conducted or funded by the agency in order to facilitate both better cooperation with others and better internal planning.** The report should be organized into broad strategic categories, with sub-categories describing program areas. Publications and other output should be listed and made available upon request.

Core Research Themes

- **The core component of EPA's research program should include three basic objectives:**

(1) Acquisition of systematic understanding about underlying environmental processes (such as those displayed in Table 2.2);
(2) Development of broadly applicable research tools, including better techniques for measuring physical, chemical, biological, social, and economic variables of interest; more accurate models of complex systems and their interactions; and new methods for analyzing, displaying, and using environmental information for science-based decision making;
(3) Design, implementation, and maintenance of appropriate environmental monitoring programs, with evaluation, analysis, synthesis and dissemination of the data and results to improve understanding of the status of and changes in environmental resources over time and to confirm that environmental policies are having the desired effect.

- **Core research projects should be selected based on their relevance to EPA's mission, whether such research is already being sponsored by other agencies, and the quality of the work proposed, as determined by a peer-review process.** Cross-cutting, interdisciplinary studies that take advantage of advances in many different fields will be particularly valuable.
- **As part of its core research efforts, EPA should conduct retrospective evaluations of the effectiveness of environmental policies and decisions.** Retrospective evaluations are critical to ensuring that environmental policies are achieving their intended goals without creating unpredicted, undesirable side-effects.
- **EPA should make a long-term financial and intellectual commitment to core research projects.** Progress in core research generally does not come quickly; therefore it is important that the agency provide adequate long-term support to this kind of knowledge development, allowing it to follow its often unpredictable course. Tool development and data collection must be ongoing endeavors in order to be fully effective.

Problem-Driven Research Themes

- **EPA should maintain a focused, problem-driven research program.** The problem-driven and core research areas will be complementary and result in the interaction of ideas and results.
- **Evaluation of problem-driven research areas should focus on reducing the risks and uncertainties associated with each problem. EPA should retain its emphasis on risk assessment to prioritize among problem-driven research areas.** Using criteria such as timing, novelty, scope, severity, and probability satisfies this requirement, as does the more detailed risk assessment framework described in the EPA strategic plan for ORD. Although risk assessment and

management provide a good framework for choosing among issues, the methodology must be refined to achieve more accurate assessments.

TABLE 5-1 Recommended Actions for EPA
- Develop and maintain a strong core research program as well as a strong problem-driven research program.
- Develop an in-house capability to identify and set priorities among current and emerging environmental issues.
- Select core research projects based on relevance to EPA's mission, coverage by others, and the quality of the proposed science.
- Conduct retrospective evaluations of the effectiveness of environmental policies and decisions.
- Make a long-term commitment to selected core research projects.
- Use criteria such as timing, novelty, scope, severity, and probability to sort important environmental issues.
- Use the risk assessment paradigm to set priorities within the problem-driven research area.
- Pay particular attention to areas where the private sector has little incentive to conduct research or develop better solutions to environmental problems.
- Re-evaluate problem-driven research priorities on a regular basis to ensure that the most important problems are being addressed.
- Increase coordination of EPA research, monitoring, and technology development activities with those of other agencies and organizations in the United States and the world.
- Ensure research personnel participation in inter-organizational coordination efforts and in scientific meetings and conferences.
- Provide a clear annual summary of the ORD research strategy and programs, organizing the programs into broad categories and identifying the value of these programs to strengthening core knowledge or solving environmental problems.

- **EPA should concentrate efforts in areas where the private sector has little incentive to conduct research or develop better solutions to environmental problems.**
- **Problem-driven research should be re-evaluated and re-focused on a regular basis to ensure that the most important problems are being addressed.** Unlike core research priorities, which may not change much over time, in the problem-driven area EPA must develop adaptive feedback capabilities to allow it to change directions when new issues arise and old issues are "solved" or judged to pose less risk than expected.

This committee was not asked to, and did not, address issues concerning EPA's research infrastructure, the appropriate balance between internal and external research, mechanisms for peer review, and other research management issues. Recommendations in these areas will be made by the Committee on Research and Peer Review at EPA (see Chapter 1). Table 5-1 summarizes recommended actions that are intended to provide EPA with the knowledge needed to address current and emerging environmental issues.

Good science is essential for sound environmental decision-making. By implementing the recommendations contained in this report, EPA can increase the effectiveness of its research program and thus continue to play an important role in efforts to protect the environment and human health into the next century.

References

Albritton, D. L., F. C. Fehsenfeld, and A. F. Tuck. 1990. Instrumental Requirements for Global Atmospheric Chemistry. Science 250(4977):75–81.

Andersson, P. S., G. J. Wasserburg, and J. Ingri. 1994. Strontium, dissolved and particulate loads in fresh and brackish waters: the Baltic Sea and Mississippi Delta. Earth Planet. Sci. Lett. 124 (1): 195–210.

Bush, V. 1945. Science: The Endless Frontier. Washington, D.C.: National Science Foundation.

Carlin A., P. F. Scodary, and D. H. Garner. 1992. Environmental investments: The cost of cleaning up. Environment 34(2):12–20, 38–44.

Carnegie Commission. 1992. Environmental Research and Development: Strengthening the Federal Infrastructure.

Elmore, D., and F. M. Phillips. 1987. Accelerator mass-spectrometry for measurement of long-lived radioisotopes. Science 236(4801):543–550.

Ellington, A. D., and J. W. Szostak. 1992. Selection in vitro of single-stranded DNA molecules that fold into specific ligand-binding structures. Nature 355:850–852.

Freudenburg, W. 1988. Perceived risk, real risk: social science and the art of probabilistic risk assessment. Science 242:44–49.

Giver, L., D. P. Bartel, M. L. Zapp, M. R. Green, and A. D. Ellington. 1993. Selection and design of high-affinity RNA ligands for HIV-1. Gene 137:19–24.

Gorham, E. 1996. Lakes under a three-pronged attack. Nature 381:109–110.

Holling, C. S. 1995. What barriers? What bridges? Pp. 14–16 in Barriers and Bridges to the Renewal of Ecosystems and Institutions, L. H. Gunderson, C. S. Holling, and S. S. Light, (eds.). New York, New York: Columbia University Press.

Hwang, S. J., T. H. Beaty, S. R. Panny, N. A. Street, J. M. Joseph, S. Gordon, I. McIntosh, and C. A. Francomano. 1995. Association study of transforming growth factor alpha (TGF alpha) Taq1 polymorphism and oral clefts: indication of gene-environment interaction in a population-based sample of infants with birth defects. Am. J. Epidemiol. 141:629–36.

Intergovernmental Panel on Climate Change (IPCC). 1996. Climate Change 1995: The Science of Climate Change: Contribution of Working Group I to the Second Assessment Report of the Intergovernmental Panel on Climate Change . J. T. Houghton, L. G. Meira Filho, B. A. Callander, N. Harris, A. Kattenberg, and K. Maskell (eds.). New York, N.Y.: Cambridge University Press.

Kates, R. W., and W. C. Clark. 1996. Environmental Surprise: Expecting the unexpected. Environment 38(2):6–12, 28–34.

Kolb, C. E. 1991. Instrumentation for chemical species measurements in the troposphere and stratosphere. Rev. of Geophys., Supplement — Proceedings of the IUGG General Assembly, 20th, Vienna, Austria, Aug. 11–24, 1991, pp. 25–36, CONF–910878.
Liu, P., Y. J. Lau, B. S. Hu, J. M. Shyr, Z. Y. Shi, W. S. Tsai, Y. H. Lin, and C. Y. Tseng. 1995. Analysis of clonal relationships among isolates of *Shigella sonnei* by different molecular typing methods. J. Clin. Microbiol. 33:1779–1783,
MITRE. 1994. Assessment of Scientific and Technical Laboratories and Facilities of the U.S. EPA.
National Academy of Public Administration. 1994. A Review, Evaluation and Critique of a Study of EPA Laboratories by the MITRE Corporation and Additional Commentary on EPA Science and Technology Programs. Washington, D.C.: National Academy of Public Administration.
National Academy of Public Administration. 1995. Setting Priorities, Getting Results: A New Direction for EPA. Washington, D.C.: National Academy of Public Administration.
National Academy of Sciences. 1996. The Ozone Depletion Phenomenon. Part of a series, Beyond Discovery: The Path from Research to Human Benefit. Washington, D.C.: National Academy Press.
National Research Council (NRC). 1983. Risk Assessment in the Federal Government: Managing the Process. Washington, D.C.: National Academy Press.
National Research Council (NRC). 1989. Irrigation-Induced Water Quality Problems. Washington, D.C.: National Academy Press.
National Research Council (NRC). 1991. Rethinking the Ozone Problem in Urban and Regional Air Pollution. Washington, D.C.: National Academy Press.
National Research Council (NRC). 1993a. Research to Protect, Restore, and Manage the Environment. Washington, D.C.: National Academy Press.
National Research Council (NRC). 1993b. Protecting Visibility in National Parks and Wilderness Areas. Washington, D.C.: National Academy Press.
National Research Council (NRC). 1994a. Alternatives for Ground Water Cleanup. Washington, D.C.: National Academy Press.
National Research Council (NRC). 1994b. Science and Judgment in Risk Assessment. Washington, D.C.: National Academy Press.
National Research Council (NRC). 1995a. Allocating Federal Funds for Science and Technology. Washington, D.C.: National Academy Press.
National Research Council (NRC). 1995b. Interim Report of the Committee on Research and Peer Review in EPA. Washington, D.C.: National Academy Press.
National Research Council (NRC). 1995c. Review of EPA's Environmental Monitoring and Assessment Program, Overall Evaluation. Washington, DC: National Academy Press.
National Research Council (NRC). 1995d. Understanding Marine Biodiversity: A Research Agenda for the Nation. Washington, D.C.: National Academy Press.
National Research Council (NRC). 1996a. Linking Science and Technology to Society's Environmental Goals. Washington, D.C.: National Academy Press.
National Research Council (NRC). 1996b. Aerosol Radiative Forcing and Climate Change. Washington, D.C.: National Academy Press.
National Research Council (NRC). 1996c. Understanding Risk: Informing Decisions in a Democratic Society. Washington, D.C.: National Academy Press.
Pasteur, L. In Familiar Quotations: A collection of passages, phrases and proverbs traced to their sources in ancient and modern literature. Edited by Emily Morison Beck. 15th edition. Boston: Little, Brown, and Company , 1980.
Russell, M. E., E. W. Colglazier, and M. R. English. 1991. Hazardous Waste Remediation: The Task Ahead. Knoxville: University of Tennessee, Waste Management and Research Institute.
Schimel, D. S., I. Enting, M. Heimann, T. M. L. Wigley, D. Raynaud, D. Alves, and U. Siegenthaler. 1995. CO_2 and the carbon cycle. In Climate Change 1994: Radiative Forcing of Climate Change and an Evaluation of the IPCC IS92 Emission Scenarios. J. T. Houghton, L. G. Meira

Filho, J. Bruce, Hoesung Lee, B. A. Callander, E. Haites, N. Harris, and K. Maskell (eds.). Cambridge, UK: Cambridge University Press.

Schindler, D. W., P. J. Curtis, B. R. Parker, and M. P. Stainton. 1996. Consequences of climate warming and lake acidification for UV-B penetration in North American boreal lakes. Nature 379(6567):705–708.

Schwartz, J. 1989. Lung function and chronic exposure to air pollution: A cross-sectional analysis of the NHANES II. Environ. Res. 50:309–321.

Schwartz, J. and D. Otto. 1987. Blood lead, hearing thresholds, and neurobehavioral development in children and youth. Arch. Environ. Health 42:153–160.

Singer, P. C. 1993. Trihalomethanes and Other Byproducts Formed by Chlorination of Drinking Water. Pp. 141–164 in M. Uman, ed. Keeping Pace with Science and Technology. Proceedings of a Symposium. Washington, D.C.: National Academy Press.

Slovic, P. 1993. Perceived risk, trust, and democracy: A systems perspective. Risk Anal. 13:675–682.

Stokes, D. E. 1995. Renewing the Compact Between Science and Government. 1995 Forum Proceedings, Vannevar Bush II — Science for the 21st Century. Pp. 15–32. Sigma XI. Research Triangle Park, NC.

Symensma, T. L., L. Giver, M. Zapp, G. B. Takle, and A. D. Ellington. 1996. RNA aptamers selected to bind human immunodeficiency virus type 1 Rev in vitro are Rev responsive in vivo. J. Virol. 70:179–187.

Teich, A. H. 1996. The federal budget and environmental priorities. Pp. 345–397 in Linking Science and Technology to Society's Environmental Goals. Washington, D.C.: National Academy Press.

Tilman, D. 1989. Approaches and Alternatives. In Long-Term Studies in Ecology. G. E. Likens, ed. New York: Springer.

Tilman, D., and J. A. Downing. 1994. Biodiversity and stability in grasslands. Nature 367:363–365.

United Nations. 1992. Urban Agglomerations. Compiled by U.N. Department of Economic and Social Development, Population Division. U.N. Publication Number ST/ESA/SER.A/133.

U.S. Environmental Protection Agency. 1992. Safeguarding the Future: Credible Science, Credible Decisions. Expert Panel on the Role of Science at EPA. EPA/600/9-91/050.

U.S. Environmental Protection Agency. 1995. Strategic Plan for the Office of Research and Development. External Review Draft.

U.S. Environmental Protection Agency. 1996. Strategic Plan for the Office of Research and Development. Final Report.

U.S. Environmental Protection Agency/Science Advisory Board (EPA/SAB). 1988. Future Risk: Research Strategies for the 1990s. SAB-EC-88-040.

U.S. Environmental Protection Agency/Science Advisory Board (EPA/SAB). 1990. Reducing Risks: Setting Priorities and Strategies for Environmental Protection. SAB-EC-90-021.

U.S. Environmental Protection Agency/Science Advisory Board (EPA/SAB). 1994. An SAB Report: Review of the MITRE Corp. Draft Report on the EPA Laboratory Study.

U.S. Environmental Protection Agency/Science Advisory Board (EPA/SAB). 1995. Beyond the Horizon: Using Foresight to Protect the Environmental Future. SAB-EC-95-007.

Vitousek, P. M. 1994. Beyond global warming: ecology and global change. Ecology 75:1861–1876.

Vitousek, P. M, C. M. D'Antonio, L. L. Loope, and R. Westbrooks. 1996. Biological invasions as global environmental change. Am. Scient. 84:468–478.

Yan, N. D., W. Keller, N. M. Scully, D. R. S. Lean, and P. J. Dillon. 1996. Increase UV-B penetration in a lake owing to drought-induced acidification. Nature 381(6578):141–143.

APPENDIXES

APPENDIX 1

Interim Report of the Committee on Research Opportunities and Priorities for EPA

INTRODUCTION

Although the Environmental Protection Agency (EPA) has always been involved in research and development on a range of environmental and ecological issues, the Agency's action agenda historically has been driven primarily by legislation passed in response to public concerns and occasionally by court orders or threatened litigation. This has often resulted in short-term fixes and piecemeal, media-specific approaches aimed at remedying the crisis of the moment.

EPA's Office of Research and Development (ORD), with a 1995 budget of $550 million and approximately 1,900 employees, has primary responsibility for providing scientific input for the agency's decision making. Addressing the often disparate needs of EPA's regulatory and research functions has been a source of tension within ORD. There is an immediate demand for the scientific data necessary to develop environmental standards and regulations. Yet these standards and regulations must be underpinned by a long-term, comprehensive research effort that can place environmental science and engineering on a firmer footing, permit a deeper understanding of the effects over time of various regulatory approaches, develop new control strategies and technologies, and help guide EPA's priorities. Despite its experienced scientific staff, ORD has received criticism over the years regarding both how it conducts research and what kinds of research it undertakes.

Recently, the Agency has increasingly recognized the complexity of many different environmental problems that interact with each other and simultaneously affect air, water, land, plants, animals, and humans. In an era of constrained government spending, there has also been a growing need to identify and focus on the largest environmental risks. This has resulted in a re-examination of how EPA, and particularly its research arm, is organized and how it detects and addresses environmental problems.

In 1994, an EPA report, *Research, Development, and Technical Services at EPA: A New Beginning* (referred to hereafter as *A New Beginning*), launched major changes in ORD's program. The implementation of these changes is ongoing, and a new document, the draft *Strategic Plan for the Office of Research and Development* (EPA, 1995), provides specifics of the mission and goals of the "new" ORD. (ORD's history, the history of external criticism of EPA's research program, and the recent changes are more fully described in a recent NRC review of ORD [NRC, 1995a]).

ROLE OF THE NATIONAL RESEARCH COUNCIL

As one input to the reorganization process, EPA's Assistant Administrator for Research and Development, Dr. Robert Huggett, requested that the National Research Council examine the proposed changes in ORD and offer advice in two separate but related areas: research management and research content. Accordingly, the NRC established two expert committees with a small overlap in membership to ensure coordination.

The first committee, launched in late 1994, is assessing EPA's research and development structure, peer review procedures, laboratory site review procedures, and career development and performance evaluation for research staff. It issued an interim report in 1995 (NRC, 1995a) that was supportive of the changes proposed in *A New Beginning* (EPA, 1994) and it is scheduled to complete its more comprehensive review by the spring of 1997.

This committee, established in December 1995, has been asked to think creatively about ORD's research areas themselves, identifying high-priority topics that will help solve some of the nation's most pressing current and future environmental problems. Experience suggests that pursuit of these research areas may spark entirely new approaches to environmental regulation and management, although many may require relatively long time frames to yield results.

SCOPE OF INTERIM REPORT

In light of a rapidly changing budgetary and programmatic climate, ORD requested quick feedback on its recently released draft Strategic Plan (EPA, 1995) in the form of this interim report. Because this committee has met only once, and has examined a limited amount of information, the findings described here are necessarily preliminary, based in large part on the expertise and extensive experience of committee members.

FUTURE GOALS FOR THIS STUDY

The final report of this study, to be issued in the spring of 1997, will explore several broad and difficult questions. What are the most critical environmental issues facing the nation today and likely to face it in the future? What do we need to know to avoid or mitigate unwanted consequences of human actions? What significant environmental research questions need attention? Are there promising new research tools and techniques that might help answer these questions? Are we in need of new approaches to environmental research to meet current and future needs?

The committee will also look more specifically at the role ORD can and should play in addressing these questions. What kind of research is most appropriate for ORD's laboratories and staff? Should other capabilities be developed within the labs? What other institutions are conducting, or are able to conduct, the kinds of research identified as most critical? How should ORD monitor and interact with them?

This study will *not* critique past research efforts at EPA or elsewhere, or look at the kinds of research management issues being considered by its companion committee. Its gaze will stay fixed on the future, attempting to anticipate the needs of the approaching new millennium.

ASSESSMENT OF ORD'S "NEW BEGINNING" AND STRATEGIC PLAN

ORD's draft Strategic Plan demonstrates a refreshing willingness to tackle the problems identified in numerous previous internal and external evaluations (e.g., EPA/SAB 1990, 1992; MITRE, 1994; NAPA, 1995; NRC, 1993, 1995a, b). Taken together with the *New Beginning* document discussed above (EPA, 1994), several promising themes emerge. Although long-term planning is extremely difficult in the face of uncertain, inadequate, and fluctuating budgets, it is nonetheless important to undertake the effort. A strategic plan allows limited resources to be used most effectively, and clarifies to others how they will be used.

In keeping with this committee's charge, this report only comments on those aspects of the plan that directly influence the selection of research topics. The related NRC *Committee on Research and Peer Review at EPA* is examining the research management and implementation aspects of the plan.

Balance Between Long-term and Short-term Research

An important aspect of ORD's new direction is the increased emphasis on long-term, fundamental research. This shift will add to the knowledge base necessary to achieve scientifically sound, cost-effective decision making in the future. Increasing the percentage of projects with a long-term focus is also an important step towards enhancing EPA's credibility as a scientific organization and achieving ORD's goal of providing national and international leadership in environmental science and risk assessment.

Working With Others

ORD's very appropriate sense of itself as a key participant in a larger arena of environmental research is evident throughout the strategic plan. Obviously, ORD alone can not do it all. Cooperation with outside scientists and others is explicitly, and appropriately, embraced, and the option is left open to implement research priorities through in-house efforts, external grants, interagency and cooperative agreements, or contracts. Other federal agencies, such as the Department of the Interior, the National Oceanographic and Atmospheric Administration, the Department of Energy, the National Institute for Environmental Health Standards, and the National Science Foundation, and scores of outside research institutes and universities, have valuable experience and capabilities in environmental research—ORD should treat them as essential partners. By building on the expertise found in other institutions, ORD can leverage its own limited resources and achieve greater environmental benefits. (The broader question of an appropriate balance between intramural and extramural research is addressed briefly in the interim report of the NRC *Committee on Research and Peer Review* [NRC, 1995a].)

As one visible way of emphasizing the importance of partnerships, it would be appropriate for the first element of ORD's proposed Mission Statement (EPA, 1995, p.7) to be changed from "Perform research and development..." to "Perform, coordinate, integrate, and support research and development...."

The Risk Paradigm

The strategic plan's adoption of risk assessment and risk management as a unifying framework is a positive step and should result in a research program that addresses issues of greatest environmental concern first. By requiring a systematic assessment of the magnitude and severity of an environmental problem relative to the many others that may exist, this approach allows for more rational decisions to be made about resource expenditures. The risk approach is also useful in highlighting the relevance of ORD's work to practical aspects of EPA's regulatory mission.

Nevertheless, there are challenges in trying to fit every issue or research topic into this framework. EPA may have to refine the risk framework or explore different analytical approaches to incorporate some of the most challenging and complex emerging environmental issues into its agenda.

Risk Assessment Methodology

The process and application of risk assessment is continually evolving. If risk assessment is to be a cornerstone of ORD's program, research is needed to improve the quality of risk assessments, as well as to analyze the strengths and weaknesses of the underlying framework and assumptions. In addition, risk assessment models and priority setting criteria must be re-examined periodically. ORD should be active in this area of study.

Some of the research questions to be pursued come to light by considering aspects of risk assessment not adequately addressed in the current draft strategic plan. One is the question of multiple risks/multiple stressors: what are *all* of the stressors to which a given population or ecosystem is exposed and how do the stressors interact? Cumulative risks must be considered to get a true picture of the severity of a problem. Similarly, it can be misleading to calculate the risk resulting from a particular stressor without considering the context of that stress, and the different settings in which it might occur. A third missing element is the explicit assessment of alternatives. The creative consideration of potential alternatives to being exposed to a particular risk needs to be included in any risk assessment. If these alternatives are not explored up front, risk managers can find themselves unnecessarily backed into a reactive mode. The three elements mentioned above should be included in the strategic plan, particularly in Figure 1 or 2 of the plan.

Near-Term Research Priorities

The six highest-priority, near-term research issues presented by ORD in its draft strategic plan—*drinking water disinfection, human health protection, ecosystem protection, particulate matter, endocrine disrupters,* and *pollution prevention and new technologies*—are intended to be implemented by ORD's laboratories. All of these topics are worthy of investigation, but the combination of topics that are very specific (e.g., "endocrine disrupters") with those that are very broad (e.g., "human health protection" and "ecosystem protection") suggests that ORD's priority-setting process continues to need refinement. The tasks described in the plan under "endocrine disrupters" are mostly exploratory exercises to determine whether these substances pose significant risks, while the latter two topics include almost everything that EPA does. It is possible that this first round of priority setting may have been influenced more by pragmatic considerations than by a strict application of the risk analysis.

ORD should continue the process of gathering input on research themes, rethinking and refining the prioritization process, and more clearly explaining the logic behind its selection of research themes in subsequent drafts of the strategic plan. The peer-review process may be particularly valuable in this regard (NRC, 1995a).

ORD should also continue to design and implement research evaluation mechanisms as a part of its ongoing priority-setting process. This is necessary to assess whether individual projects are appropriately aligned to address important emerging problems, as well as whether ORD has achieved its overall goal of promoting long-term research.

Emerging Issues

Although the plan refers more than once to the importance of anticipating emerging issues, it does not include an approach for identifying such issues. In the absence of such an approach, these issues will not be identified early on when they may be most tractable. Although ORD's Environmental Monitoring and Assessment Program (EMAP) is one example of a program that might be helpful in providing such early warning signals, the program has proven extremely difficult to implement soundly (NRC, 1995b).

Specific criteria for identifying emerging issues were laid out in the recent report, *Beyond the Horizon* (EPA/SAB, 1995). This report calls for issues to be assessed according to their timing, novelty, scope, severity, visibility, and probability. The report's recommendations should be reviewed and ORD should identify criteria and procedures for identifying emerging issues of relevance to EPA in future drafts of the strategic plan.

Remaining Questions

A preliminary assessment such as this one necessarily leaves many questions unanswered. This committee has only begun to identify and prioritize critical research areas to be addressed by ORD and others. In addition, questions concerning ORD's strategic plan were raised, but not resolved, in the process of writing this report. These questions will continue to be addressed along with many others as this study continues.

CONCLUSION

ORD has taken important steps towards improving the conduct and content of its research program. The *New Beginning* (EPA, 1994) and ORD's draft Strategic Plan (EPA, 1995) indicate an awareness of the importance of long-term fundamental research in understanding and ameliorating complex environmental problems. ORD's emphasis on cooperation with other institutions is also very important. By taking advantage of the nation's most capable scientists, wherever they may be working, and encouraging new generations of researchers, ORD can leverage its own resources enormously.

ORD's adoption of risk assessment as a unifying framework for evaluating problems and setting priorities holds promise for producing a more consistent, rational, relevant, and defensible research program. However, if risk assessment is to be the cornerstone of ORD's program, an ongoing research program should be undertaken to continuously refine, improve, and evaluate the risk assessment methodology and to identify situations where it should be supplemented with other approaches.

In order to devote limited resources to the most important problems, ORD should continue to refine its priority setting process so that it can clearly explain its choice of short- and long-term focus areas. A system for identifying potentially important emerging issues should also be developed and implemented.

This committee's final report will attempt to identify and prioritize critical research issues and will discuss the roles to be played by ORD and others in addressing them.

REFERENCES

EPA. 1994. *Research, Development, and Technical Services at EPA: A New Beginning.* EPA/600/R-94/122.

EPA. 1995. *Strategic Plan for the Office of Research and Development.* November 1995, External Review Draft. EPA/600/R-95/162.

EPA/SAB. 1990. *Reducing Risk: Setting Priorities and Strategies for Environmental Protection.* EPA-SAB-EC-90-021.

EPA/SAB. 1992. *Safeguarding the Future: Credible Science, Credible Decisions.* EPA-SAB-EC-92-005.

EPA/SAB. 1995. *Beyond the Horizon: Using Foresight to Protect the Environmental Future.* EPA-SAB-EC-95-007.

MITRE. 1994. *Assessment of Scientific and Technical Laboratories and Facilities of the U.S. Environmental Protection Agency.* McLean, Virginia. MTR 94W0000082V1.

NAPA. 1995. *Setting Priorities, Getting Results: A New Direction for EPA.* National Academy of Public Administration. Washington, D.C.

NRC. 1993. *Research to Protect, Restore, and Manage the Environment.* National Academy Press. Washington, D.C.

NRC. 1995a. *Interim Report of the Committee on Research and Peer Review in EPA.* National Academy Press. Washington, D.C.

NRC. 1995b. *Review of EPA's Environmental Monitoring and Assessment Program: An Overall Evaluation.* National Academy Press. Washington, D.C.

APPENDIX 2

Reports Analyzed to Identify Priority Environmental Issues

1. National Research Council (NRC). 1996. Carcinogens and Anticarcinogens in the Human Diet. Washington, D.C.: National Academy Press.
2. National Research Council (NRC). 1996. Hazardous Materials in the Hydrologic Environment. Washington, D.C.: National Academy Press.
3. National Research Council (NRC). 1996. Linking Science and Technology to Society's Environmental Goals. Washington, D.C.: National Academy Press.
4. National Research Council (NRC). 1996. A Plan for a Research Program on Aerosol Radiative Forcing and Climate Change. Washington, D.C.: National Academy Press.
5. National Research Council (NRC). 1996. Understanding The Bering Sea Ecosystem. Washington, D.C.: National Academy Press.
6. NSF (National Science Foundation). 1996. Environmental Geochemistry and Biogeochemistry: Research at the Interfaces of Geochemistry, Hydrology, Coastal Sciences, Chemistry, Microbial and Molecular Biology, Colloid and Transport Engineering, and Mathematics.
7. EPA/SAB (U.S. Environmental Protection Agency/Science Advisory Board). 1995. Beyond the Horizon: Using Foresight to Protect the Environmental Future. SAB-EC-95-007.
8. Gas Research Institute. 1995. Environmental Trends and Issues at the Research Horizon: Outlook for the Twenty-First Century.
9. IPCC (Intergovernmental Panel on Climate Change). 1995. The IPCC Second Assessment Report, Vols. I and II, Cambridge University Press, Cambridge, England.
10. Naiman, R. J., J. J. Magnuson, D. M. McKnight, and J. A. Stanford. 1995. The Freshwater Imperative: A Research Agenda. Island Press, Washington, D.C. 165 pp.

11. NRC (National Research Council). 1995. Review of the EPA's Environmental Monitoring and Assessment Program. Washington, D.C.: National Academy Press.
12. NRC (National Research Council). 1995. Understanding Marine Biodiversity: A Research Agenda for the Nation. Washington, D.C.: National Academy Press.
13. WMO (World Meteorological Organization). 1995. Scientific Assessment of Ozone Depletion: 1994. Global Ozone Research and Monitoring Project. Report No. 37. WMO, Geneva, Switzerland. 508 pp.
14. NRC (National Research Council). 1994. Priorities for Coastal Ecosystem Science. Washington, D.C.: National Academy Press.
15. NRC (National Research Council). 1993. Pesticides in the Diets of Infants and Children. Washington, D.C.: National Academy Press.
16. NRC (National Research Council). 1993. Research to Protect, Restore, and Manage the Environment. Washington, D.C.: National Academy Press.
17. NRC (National Research Council). 1993. Solid-Earth Sciences and Society. Washington, D.C.: National Academy Press.
18. EPA/SAB (U.S. Environmental Protection Agency/Science Advisory Board). 1992. Safeguarding the Future: Credible Science, Credible Decisions. Expert Panel on the Role of Science at EPA. EPA/600/9-91/050.
19. NRC (National Research Council). 1992. Science and the National Parks. Washington, D.C.: National Academy Press.
20. Lubchenco, J., A. M. Olson, L. B. Brubaker, S. R. Carpenter, M. M. Holland, S. P. Hubbell, S. A. Levin, J. A. MacMahon, P. A. Matson, J. M. Melillo, H. A. Mooney, C. H. Peterson, H. R. Pulliam, L. A. Real, P. J. Regal, and P. G. Risser. 1991. The Sustainable Biosphere Initiative: An Ecological Research Agenda. Ecology 72(2), pp. 371-412.
21. NRC (National Research Council). 1991. Opportunities in the Hydrologic Sciences. Washington, D.C.: National Academy Press.
22. NRC (National Research Council). 1991. Rethinking the Ozone Problem in Urban and Regional Air Pollution. Washington, D.C.: National Academy Press.
23. EPA/SAB (U.S. Environmental Protection Agency/Science Advisory Board). 1990. Reducing Risk: Setting Priorities and Strategies for Environmental Protection. SAB-EC-90-021.
24. EPA/SAB (U.S. Environmental Protection Agency/Science Advisory Board). 1988. Future Risk: Research Strategies for the 1990s. SAB-EC-88-040.

APPENDIX 3

Biographical Sketches of Committee Members

RAYMOND C. LOEHR, *Chair*, has been the H. M. Alharthy Centennial Chair and professor of civil engineering at The University of Texas in Austin since 1985. Previous to this appointment, he taught environmental engineering and had major research programs at Case Institute of Technology, University of Kansas, and Cornell University. He is a former chair of EPA's Science Advisory Board and presently a member of the Board on Environmental Studies and Toxicology. Dr. Loehr obtained B.S. and M.S. degrees from the Case Institute of Technology, and a Ph.D. in sanitary engineering from the University of Wisconsin. He has been a member of the National Academy of Engineering since 1983.

SANDRA ARCHIBALD is associate dean and associate professor at the Hubert H. Humphrey Institute of Public Affairs, University of Minnesota. Prior to these appointments, she taught at the Food Research Institute of Standford University. Dr. Archibald obtained her B.A. and M.S. degrees in public policy from the University of California, Berkeley, and M.S. and Ph.D. degrees in agricultural economics from the University of California, Davis.

JOHN I. BRAUMAN is the J. G. Jackson - C. J. Wood Professor of Chemistry at Stanford University, where he has taught since 1963. His research interests are in organic chemistry and physical chemistry; gas-phase ionic reactions and spectroscopy; visible and infrared spectroscopy and photochemistry; electron photo-detachment spectroscopy; and reaction mechanism. He obtained his B.S. from the Massachusetts Institute of Technology and his Ph.D. from the University of California, Berkeley. He has been a member of the National Academy of Sciences since 1976.

JOHN D. BREDEHOEFT retired in 1994 as deputy assistant chief research hydrologist at the Water Resources Division of the U.S. Geological Survey after 32 years of service. He now runs his own consulting firm, the HYDRODYNAMICS Group. At the USGS, he engaged in both research and high-level management. He managed the entire USGS water research activities for five years in the 1970s, and was the regional manager for all USGS water activities (regional hydrologist) in eight western states for four years in the early 1980s. He received his B.S.E. from Princeton University and his M.S. and Ph.D. in geology from the University of Illinois. He is a member of the National Academy of Engineering and the Russian Academy of Natural Sciences.

GEORGE P. DASTON is currently the principal research scientist in developmental and reproductive toxicology at the Miami Valley Laboratory of the Procter & Gamble Company in Ohio. Concurrently, he is an adjunct associate professor of pediatrics at the Children's Hospital Research Foundation at the University of Cincinnati. His research interests are developmental biology; teratology and toxicology, especially mechanisms of normal and abnormal development; nutrient-toxicant interactions; in vitro alternatives in teratology and toxicology; functional teratology; fluid balance in development; and risk assessment. He received his B.S. and Ph.D. in developmental biology and teratology from the University of Miami.

KENNETH L. DEMERJIAN is director of the Atmospheric Sciences Research Center and professor of atmospheric science at the State University of New York at Albany. His research interests include the chemistry and mechanistic processes of clean and polluted troposphere; kinetic and mechanistic pathway studies of atmospheric species; computer models for simulating air quality and atmospheric processes; and instrumentation development for the measurement of trace atmospheric constituents. He holds a B.S. from Northeastern University and an M.S. and a Ph.D. in physical chemistry from Ohio State University.

NINA V. FEDOROFF is the Willaman Professor of Life Sciences and director of the Biotechnology Institute at Pennsylvania State University. Dr. Fedoroff's research areas are plant transposable elements, epigenetic mechanisms, and plant development. She holds a B.S. in biology and chemistry from Syracuse University and a Ph.D. in molecular biology from Rockefeller University. She has been a member of the National Academy of Sciences since 1990.

ROLF HARTUNG is professor of environmental toxicology at the University of Michigan in Ann Arbor. His research interests include effects of polluting oils on waterfowl; toxicity of aminoethanols; coactions between chlorinated hydrocarbon.

pesticides and aquatic pollutants; environmental dynamics of heavy metals; and risk assessment. He received his B.S., M.W.M., and Ph.D. in wildlife management from the University of Michigan.

JAMES F. HAYS retired in 1995 as director of the Division of Earth Sciences at the National Science Foundation (NSF). Prior to joining the NSF in 1982, he was professor of geology and chair of the Department of Geological Sciences at Harvard University. Dr. Hays's research interests are experimental petrology and the petrology of lunar and terrestrial igneous rocks. He was a principal investigator in the Apollo lunar sample program and has served as advisor to the National Aeronautics and Space Administration, U.S. Geological Survey, Bureau of Mines, Forest Service, Department of Energy, and the National Academy of Sciences. He received his A.B. from Columbia University, M.S. from the California Institute of Technology, and Ph.D. from Harvard.

CHARLES E. KOLB is president and chief executive officer of Aerodyne Research, Inc., in Massachusetts. At Aerodyne since 1971, his principal research interests have included atmospheric chemistry, combustion chemistry, chemical lasers, materials chemistry, and the chemical physics of rocket and aircraft exhaust plumes. He has served on a variety of National Research Council committees dealing with environmental issues, chaired the Committee on Atmospheric Chemistry, and serves on the Board on Atmospheric Sciences and Climate. He received his S.B. in chemical physics from the Massachusetts Institute of Technology and his M.A. and Ph.D. in physical chemistry from Princeton University.

JUDITH MCDOWELL is a senior scientist and coordinator of the Woods Hole Oceanographic Institution's Sea Grant Program. Her research works are in the areas of comparative physiology of marine larval and post larval crustaceans, including studies of energetics and nutrition; coastal pollution; and the effects of pollutants on the physiology of marine animals. Dr. McDowell is a member of the National Research Council's Commission on Geosciences, Environment, and Resources. She received a B.S. in biology from Stonehill College and an M.S. and Ph.D. in zoology from the University of New Hampshire.

JUDITH MEYER is a professor at the Institute of Ecology, University of Georgia. Her expertise is in stream ecology, and her research includes nutrient dynamics in stream ecosystems, with emphasis on dissolved organic carbon and phosphorus; ecosystem analysis of blackwater rivers; effects of watershed disturbance on aquatic ecosystems; functional assessment of urban streams; and role of riparian zones in controlling nonpoint pollution sources. She has served on several National Research Council committees and is a former member of the Water Science and Technology Board. She obtained her B.S. from the University of Michigan, M.S. from the University of Hawaii, and Ph.D. in ecology and evolutionary biology from Cornell University.

CHARLES RICHARD O'MELIA is currently a professor in the Department of Geography and Environmental Engineering at the Johns Hopkins University. Dr. O'Melia's professional experience includes positions at Hazen & Sawyer Engineers; University of Michigan; Georgia Institute of Technology; Harvard University; and the University of North Carolina in Chapel Hill. His research interests are in aquatic chemistry, environmental fate and transport, predictive modeling of natural systems, and theory of water and wastewater treatment. He received a B.C.E. from Manhattan College and an M.S.E. and Ph.D. in sanitary engineering from the University of Michigan. Dr. O'Melia has been a member of the National Academy of Engineering since 1989.

GARY WILLIAMS is director of the Naylor Dana Institute and chief of the Division of Pathology and Toxicology, American Health Foundation. He is also a research professor in the Department of Pathology, New York Medical College. Dr. Williams is editor of *Cell Biology and Toxicology* and also serves on the editorial boards of *Toxicologic Pathology, Drug and Chemical Toxicology, Archives of Toxicology*, and *Nutrition and Cancer*. His research fields are the genetic, toxic and carcinogenic effects of chemicals, on which he has over 410 publications. He received his B.A. from Washington and Jefferson College and his M.D. from the University of Pittsburgh School of Medicine.

ROY WOLFE is associate director of water quality at the Metropolitan Water District of Southern California. Previously, he has been associated with the University of California, Irvine. He has had 15 years of experience in water quality, with particular emphasis on microbiology. He received a B.A. in zoology from San Diego State University and a Ph.D. in environmental science from the University of California, Irvine.

LILY YOUNG is a professor at the Center for Agricultural Molecular Biology and the Department of Environmental Science at Cook College, Rutgers University. Formerly, Dr. Young taught at Stanford University and at the New York University Medical Center. She has served on various review and oversight panels including two other National Research Council committees, one for the Marine Board and one for the Naval Board. She obtained a B.S. and an M.S. in bacteriology from Cornell University and a Ph.D. in environmental microbiology from Harvard University.

THOMAS ZOSEL is manager for environmental initiatives at 3M's Corporate Environmental Technology and Services Department. He currently serves on EPA's Clean Air Act Advisory Committee and chairs the National Pollution Prevention Center Advisory Board. He was past chair of the American Institute of Chemical Engineers' Center for Waste Reduction Technologies. He received a B.S. in chemical engineering from the University of Wisconsin.

Staff

MORGAN GOPNIK, study director, is assistant director of the Commission on Geosciences, Environment, and Resources and director of the Ocean Studies Board at the National Research Council. She received a B.Sc. in physical geography from McGill University and an M.S. in environmental engineering science from the California Institute of Technology.